Maybe I Can
Rise Above
A Story For The Misunderstood
Volume 1

Saffire-Rose
Fletcher

First published by Busybird Publishing 2021

Copyright © 2021 Saffire Rose-Fletcher

ISBN: 978-1-922465-63-4

This work is copyright. Apart from any use permitted under the *Copyright Act 1968*, no part of this publication may be reproduced, stored in a retrieval system or transmitted in any form or by any means, electronic, mechanical, photocopying, recording or otherwise, without the prior written permission of Saffire Rose-Fletcher.

Cover Image: Saffire-Rose Fletcher

Cover design: Busybird Publishing

Layout and typesetting: Busybird Publishing

Busybird Publishing
2/118 Para Road
Montmorency, Victoria
Australia 3094
www.busybird.com.au

I dedicate this book to my mother.

- Saffire

About the Author

Saffire-Rose Fletcher was born on the central coast of Australia in 1986.

She embarked on her journey as a singer/songwriter in 2013, turning her poems into songs, combining that with her (brief) piano knowledge, while also studying audio engineering and sound production.

Her lecturer identified that she had talent and that she was somebody to watch in the future.

As a means of further developing her craft, she used the open mic night scene as a training ground. It was a challenging period but also invaluable experience.

In 2015, Saffire moved to Melbourne (the musical capital of Australia) to pursue her dream of becoming an established and successful singer/songwriter.

Since then, Saffire has played over 250 gigs, recorded countless demos, directed and filmed her music videos, and has varied her musical genres by exploring the rock scene with her band 'SAFFIRE'.

It wasn't until late 2018, when Saffire discovered her true sound, which resembles EDM qualities.

Saffire's intention through her songs is to address topics that are overlooked in society – primarily in the realm of self-development, grief, forgiveness, self-love and, most of all, combatting adversity.

She has since become a qualified counselor, has embarked on some acting endeavours and has become a published author of two books: *Maybe I Can Rise Above* and *Revive My Life*.

Follow Saffire on Instagram, Twitter, YouTube, Tiktok and Facebook in order to find out more about her, her music, her two published books and where to purchase them.

Facebook:
www.facebook.com/saffireroseofficial/

Instagram:
www.instagram.com/saffirerosefletcher_official

Spotify:
open.spotify.com/artist/14xr80t6QNIrKCXxxdJmNA

Tiktok:
tiktok.com/@saffirerosefletcher

Twitter:
https://twitter.com/officialsaffire

YouTube:
www.YouTube.com/saffirerosefletcher

Contents

Introduction	1
Chapter 1 **The Beginning**	7
Chapter 2 **Education**	17
Chapter 3 **Not Your Average Adolescence**	25
Chapter 4 **Identity Crisis**	35
Chapter 5 **They Never Warn You**	47
Chapter 6 **Learning The Hard Way**	57
Chapter 7 **A Downward Spiral**	69
Chapter 8 **Awakening**	79
Chapter 9 **Losing Everything**	89
Chapter 10 **It Gets Worse**	99
Chapter 11 **Growing Pains**	113
Chapter 12 **Perspective**	127
Chapter 13 **2020**	133
Acknowledgements	141
Resources	143

Introduction

This is not a self-help book. This is a story about understanding damaged people, about self-acceptance, overcoming adversity and learning to love who you are, no matter what you've been through.

Hi, my name is Saffire and boy have I lived a life. I've written this book in order to help others feel less alone with their thoughts, experiences and emotions.

The world can be hard to process at times, and when we're surrounded by so many different opinions and values it can get a little bit confusing. After all, everyone is contending with a different life to lead. We are born into this world with our own set of circumstances and we're expected to have all the answers straight away. Let's be realistic, we have no idea who we are and what we need in our lives, unless we go through the process of eliminating the things we don't want.

In this book I'll be covering all sorts of adversities you can experience in a lifetime, and how those issues can ultimately impact people in terms of their overall wellbeing. I'll also illustrate how the opinions and judgements of others can influence your perception of yourself, and how this can ultimately prevent you from loving yourself and attracting what you deserve.

I'll share some candid reflections from my own personal experiences, and the factors that contribute toward how a person can be so fundamentally misunderstood. I myself had been diagnosed with complex post-traumatic syndrome disorder (PTSD) in the midst of Covid-19, adding to the reality that my musical dream was coming to an end. Luckily I had a back-up plan as a qualified counsellor – but I still had to work on myself before I could dare to help others.

This is a story about my process of healing and the obstacles I've encountered along the way. I spent four years writing this book, trying to understand what I was writing about. Now I know I was writing about the unknown, and being okay with not having the answers; learning to accept my failures and embrace some amazing possibilities. It inspired me to want to help, help anyone I could – even just through sharing my own experiences: my fears, my hang-ups and downfalls. I want people to feel less ashamed for going through their own growing pains. I mean, how do we learn unless we make a few mistakes? How do we find out what we want and who we truly are if we don't learn some harsh lessons first?

In each of my relationships, the opinions of others coloured my perception of myself, and this meant I didn't feel I was enough, which led to all sorts of issues and eventually the breakdown of those relationships as I navigated the growing pains of becoming who I am. In this way, each relationship became a stepping stone to accepting myself.

The lesson I needed to learn, that we all need to learn, is that I am enough. I was always enough. No matter what's happened or what you've been through, you are always enough.

This is what I went through, and this is how it led to me becoming who I am, accepting who I am – healing from the past and overcoming what I've been through.

This story is about meeting those who need healing, and meeting them where they're at. So let's heal together.

Chapter 1

The Beginning

I was born on the 27th of July, 1986, on the Central Coast of Australia. Mum gave birth to me at the ripe old age of 42 years old.

Mum was a single parent leaving behind a chaotic life. She had no possessions, no financial assistance from my father and no support system. She had very little self-awareness – only her intuition and her emotional triggers as she took on the unknown.

The first suburb that Mum and I lived in together was Budgewoi. It was within reasonable distance of the famous coastal beaches. Our stay was short lived, though, as Mum was approved for a housing commission in a suburb called Tumbi Umbi. Prior to the relocation, I recall Mum crying as she stood at the top of the stairs of our new townhouse. 'This doesn't feel right,' she said. Her intuition would be validated as the years passed.

We moved into what some titled 'The Butter Box', a small two-storey brick house surrounded by other townhouses. The street was an oval shape. It was an intimate neighbourhood, with very little privacy.

For Christmas and other festivities it would just be Mum and I. Our Christmas tree would be surrounded by modest gifts that Mum could barely afford. I suspect Mum was trying to compensate for the lack of acknowledgement from our family, including my Dad.

I don't remember much about my father, but one of the most prominent memories I have was of him sitting on a bed with tears in his eyes. I was five. He said to Mum, 'If anyone ever hurts her, I'll kill them.'

The conviction in his passionate statement proved to be a poor representation of his future actions, though, as he suddenly disappeared afterwards. He then never attempted to get in touch or rectify the confusion his disappearance caused me as a child. I remember Mum crying over him a lot. She spoke of him fondly, despite his absence and lack of financial assistance.

Mum told me that my father had never wanted kids – though Mum proceeded to have me regardless. I know that it 'takes two to tango,' but I can understand the situation from both perspectives. I don't condone a father abandoning his child – but he did warn my mother prior to the conception that he didn't want kids, and she deliberately avoided taking the pill. He also tried to remain present during my childhood. I'll give him that.

I don't resent him for leaving, despite the fact that Mum and I struggled. We both became stronger for it! I try to view things from a more constructive viewpoint in order to justify the loss. Call me soft – but hey, it's how I cope.

Mum did the best she could. There were little things she did to try and give me a normal childhood. For example, a tooth fairy named 'Flutter-bye' would collect my teeth whenever they fell out, and I'd wake up to five dollars underneath my pillow.

When I was five, Mum and I fought like cats and dogs. In my youthful angst, I didn't know how to gain control over tense situations. I'd resort to punching holes in the wall and screaming at the top of my lunges. Sometimes I'd even pretend to faint in order to snap her out of her antics.

Mum would project some of her past negative experiences onto me. Hey, she had no one to talk to, and she hadn't addressed some of her underlying issues. How was she to know? At the time, I just thought she wanted to challenge everything I suggested, but I was wrong. We were just two different people, coming from two different perspectives – attempting to come together.

Our arguments would continue for many years, but we'd kiss and make up for the most part. She was my best friend. It wasn't until my late twenties that I started to understand her better, but prior to establishing where Mum was coming from, I held great resentment towards her for us not having a family, and for the negative stories she'd share with me regarding her past. I mean, I learned what rape was at the age of five.

My friendships were also compromised because Mum would argue it wasn't safe for me to go for sleepovers with friends, which is fair enough ... though Mum had me catching buses by myself to the local shopping centre at the age of twelve, having trained me to get her groceries and to pay her bills once a week. I never understood the logic, especially in the realm of 'protection', as it was a total contradiction to her fear of my sleepovers. Mum assured me (in relation to me doing her shopping at such a young age) that she was merely trying to prepare me in case I ever became an orphan. Geez, that's comforting.

All jokes aside, my childhood was unique to say the least. Yeah, I grew up fast. I was constantly anticipating the worst, and our neighbourhood dramas only caused me more distress.

When I look back, I feel like Mum placed restrictions on my friendships because she didn't want to be left alone. I can understand this as I consequently grew up with similar fears myself. I can therefore empathise with how a person can become co-dependent. It's a vicious cycle. Even grown adults aren't immune to 'FOMO' or the fear of missing out. Just because you're co-dependent doesn't make you psychotic ... it's simply a fear of being left behind! I think we've all had at least one moment in our lives where we've struggled with these kinds of feelings. After all, we're human – though in my adolescence I didn't have the mental and emotional capacity in order to understand this, so of course I fought against it.

It wasn't all bad, though. I recall one precious memory I'll always hold close to my heart. I remember, at the age of five, that I chucked a fit in the lolly section of a convenient store. I demanded candy! (Depriving me of confectionery was never wise.)

Mum looked around at all the other customers and asked, 'Does anybody own this child?' I responded, in my utterly confused state, 'I belongs to you.' Mum smiled and bought my candy.

Anyway, there were some good things about my neighbourhood. I made a couple of friends, and we fell off our bikes a lot! (You've got to love the bonding rituals of children). I had stitches in my chin due to falling off my training bike at age four. I jammed my right hand in my neighbour's car door at age eight. And I got chicken pox at age eleven. I thought the worst of my life was over. What a rude awakening I had to come to later on!

It's when I look back to the age of nine, though, that the memories are the most prominent. Most weeks Mum and I were so incredibly broke that we'd be eating out of Vegemite jars for days. By the time pay day arrived, my stomach had already shrunken to the point where I was no longer hungry and I'd be vomiting bile.

But the one event that truly impacted my childhood would be an unexpected visit from a couple of Mum's relatives, who came to stay with Mum and I for ten days. Mum's side of the family had been practically non-existent due to petty feuds and a misguided perception of my mother. Reforming a connection was highly ambitious, and I can see that now in hindsight. But at the time, the failed attempt at reconnecting and having them leave had a significant impact on my abandonment issues.

As I look back on this chapter of my life, I understand why they couldn't stay. They'd been through hell, and attempting to reconcile with Mum after all they'd been through was just too much.

Mum also had a very old friend in her life. He was like a grandfather to me – but contact with him was inconsistent and not without consequences. As I grew into a teenager, he made a move on me (more on that later). This inevitably tainted my view of him.

The second incident that impacted me greatly was the discovery of countless letters that had been sent to our home address, detailing the intention to kidnap and rape me after school. This commenced between the ages of nine and twelve.

Our neighbourhood had it in for my mother. They'd walk past our house literally throwing stones as they proceeded to call her a witch. I believe my mother was targeted because she was a single parent who kept to herself – while everyone else in the neighbourhood wanted to drink, take drugs, argue until they saw blood, and sleep with each other's partners.

I saw things that a child should never be subjected to.

The main friendship I kept during my younger years would be with a girl called Sam, my next-door neighbour. We dreamed of being popstars and we'd perform mini concerts outside my house for the neighbours to see. In all honesty, though, most of the adults were sleeping off their hangovers during the daytime.

At the end of the oval there was nothing but bushland, with a wooden fence poorly attempting to protect us children from our own curiosity. A story arose regarding one of my friends named Jenna. It was suggested that she had been attacked in that very bush. I never found out what truly happened – but still to this day, I hope she's okay. I recall Jenna returning to the street in my early teenage years to reconnect with me. I neglected to ask about those stories, something I still regret. She disappeared not long after that meeting.

Just to throw a spanner in the works, at the age of thirteen I started to notice that Mum's left arm was forming pink bubbly skin around a large indentation of a wound. It eventually turned into a massive gaping hole and I noticed traces of blood in the shower.

Mum sat me down one day and told me that she suspected that she had cancer. She didn't want to get it formally diagnosed, as she'd recently lost a friend to cancer. (Mum's friend had warned her that it's the *knowing* that is the killer.) Mum refrained from ever visiting a doctor's surgery from that point onwards.

Mum and I just carried on with our lives as if nothing was wrong, but deep down, I was developing a massive fear of becoming an orphan at any minute. Looking back, I can see this was part of my complex PTSD – though my fears were merited, as Mum refused to see a doctor. My biggest fear was waking up one day to see her dead body and having nowhere to go.

Chapter 2

Education

Primary school consisted of me being pushed, shoved and bullied for being 'povo' (or poor), and for my lack of attendance to school. My mind was filled with fears of being kidnapped and raped, teachers telling me how stupid and disappointing I was, and constantly being threatened by bullies.

I made many excuses to Mum as to why I didn't want to attend school. As a result, Mum received many visits from a School Liaison officer with concerns for my welfare.

I remember, at the age of nine, I resorted to faking my period. I had an unusual method of biting the inside of my mouth until it bled, then I sucked the blood and placed it onto my pants. What can I say, I was desperate.

On one particular occasion, one of the teachers was becoming suspicious of my absence from school and questioned my story regarding 'my period'. I suspected that I'd be questioned, so I strategically prepared my evidence ahead of time. She asked me to stand in the corner of the classroom (after all the children had left) and asked me to pull down my pants in order to prove my innocence. I understand that I was lying, and I take ownership of my actions. But I was just a child! A teacher going to this extent to prove that I was guilty was just ludicrous! I mean, why not just get to the bottom of *why* a child is too scared to attend school, instead of painting a child as a 'problem'?

Regardless, through the years I became known as a 'problem child'. I guess some of teachers had their own opinions about me. I got yelled at a lot for the most unjustifiable reasons. My nervous system became weak and, as a result, I ended up wetting my pants in the classroom on various occasions. I had teachers telling me that I was filthy and hopeless and, to add fuel to the fire, the bullying exceeded beyond my ability to cope.

One day I was walking home from school and I'd held onto my bladder for a significant amount of time. One of my most prominent bullies was walking behind me. All of a sudden, a magpie swooped down onto me to attack! I'd seen what these birds could do … needless to say, I was terrified. In my attempt to run away and dodge the bird, I wet my pants. I was a thirteen year old urinating in public.

'Oh my god, Saffire just wet her pants,' the bully proceeded to laugh and point at my misfortune. I was mortified!

The most distressing occurrence of bullying that I endured, though, was being pushed into the deep end of a school carnival pool. I reached the bottom of the pool and kept drowning, bobbing back up to the top four times in under thirty seconds. I couldn't swim or breathe. Luckily, a teacher jumped in and pulled me out.

Did I mention that those bullies also attempted to torch half of the school, and almost succeeded? Geez, I wonder why I resorted to such an unorthodox method to avoid school …

During my school years, my home life wasn't entirely safe either, as many neighbourhood disturbances broke out in our street. One particular evening, a woman ripped our garage door off its hinges. Then, the following week, Sam and I were walking our bikes home to discover two grown men punching each other to death. Blood was everywhere.

I became very aware of the dangers that surrounded me. I couldn't just be a kid and relax. I was hypersensitive to every possible hazard. On a nightly basis I'd walk around the house on eggshells. I'd peer out of the main window for any signs of trouble. I felt like I had to be Mum's protector. I recall writing a letter to God, pleading, 'Please protect my mum and me from any danger.'

It was also around this time that I started having vivid dreams of girls around my age. The dreams were very innocent and generally involved me leaning in for a kiss. These dreams commenced long before my teenage years. To add to my confusion, I started to develop a crush on my next-door neighbour Sam, but I never told her.

Hobbie-wise, I started to develop an interest in dancing and singing, though Mum couldn't afford the classes.

Finally, my primary school days were over and I was about to embark on my new journey of high school! Within the first week of my attendance, I made a drastic attempt in order to be liked. I noticed that some of the popular girls were eyeing off my pink fluffy pencil case that Mum had bought me from a cheap discount store. It was the only ice-breaker I could think of.

I made a poor decision, fabricating a story that my aunty was manager of the store that sold these, and proceeded to tell them I could get them similar pencil cases. They were eager to oblige and treated me as an equal until it became abundantly clear that I was lying. With each day that passed, I kept on making excuses as to why I'd failed to bring what was promised to school. Needless to say, those excuses had reached an expiry date. By succumbing to this kind of approach, I think it's safe to say I had no confidence in my ability to make friends.

Everything got worse. The main bully from my old primary school resurfaced at high school. She lived close to where I got off the bus on a Thursday afternoon after finishing Mum's shopping. One afternoon, she ran up to me with one of her friends, demanding that I give her whatever money was left over from Mum's groceries.

At school I'd been slapped across the face, farted on, sworn at, had money thrown at me because I was poor, and told constantly I was dumb and fat. If I won an award (which only happened once), it was due to sheer luck!

The only good memory I recall from during this time was spending time with my new friend, Terrie. Staying at her place was the only positive escape I had from it all. She had 'the life' – a loving mother and father, and a beautiful home in a wonderful neighbourhood. It was the only time that I could close my eyes and rest peacefully… despite the hesitance from Mum at times to let me sleep over.

The bullying became so unbearable that I decided to leave high school at the age of fourteen and join the workforce. I left everything behind, and ignored Terrie's calls as I felt embarrassed for being a high school drop-out.

I just want to state that not everything was negative during this time. I came across some wonderful teachers and principals during my school years. The only thing lacking was emotional and mental support for students coming from a difficult background, who were contending with different social complexities. This has indeed improved over the years. My only intention here is to explain my version of events in order to tell this story.

Chapter 3

Not Your Average Adolescence

Just weeks after leaving high school, I started working for a café close to home. I'd work five days a week, 7am – 4pm. I became one of the best baristas in the shop … I was in my element!

I started to develop a crush on one of the girls who worked there. Her name was Mary, and she was my supervisor. Oh did I have it bad for her … I was obsessed! We'd be invited to work parties and I'd usually end up spending most the night awkwardly staring at her in awe. I really liked her. To my disappointment, though, Mary scored herself a boyfriend later that year. I was heartbroken, but appeared unaffected in order to maintain my position with my employer.

Nevertheless, I did make some new friends at work. To my surprise, one of the girls appeared to like me. It was never confirmed, but sometimes you just know. On one occasion, this girl drove me home after I finished work. I had my period and I had no pads in my bag. So what happened? I accidentally bled on her car seat. Once she dropped me off I asked her to wait as I nervously ran inside, then ran back with a damp cloth and attempted to pat off the blood before it stained her car seat. She awkwardly said, 'Saff, it's okay,' then drove off. I avoided eye contact with her for a while and that connection quickly faded.

Oh to be human … it's a glorious thing, especially in your teenage years. Nothing could be worse, right? Haha.

My sixteenth birthday was coming up and my boss offered to throw me a party at her house on the condition that I'd pay for the food.

A week before my birthday bash, I called my father for the first time and invited him along. I hadn't spoken to him since I was five years old. He replied, 'I don't think that would be appropriate.' As a consequence, I felt utterly embarrassed and rejected – though remained polite and told him, 'It's okay, I understand,' then hung up. Granted, in hindsight I can see that it would've been awkward for him to appear at a party full of strangers, especially after all those years.

Nevertheless my birthday was great, minus a couple of hiccups. Mum literally had no one to invite (I think she might've been concerned about what my boss and her crew thought), so invited some of our neighbours, who caused us a lot of trouble.

Later on that year, my manager sold her business and two new managers (a husband and wife from Greece) took over the shop. Not long after my previous manager's departure, the new managers grew fond of me rather quickly, especially the husband. He praised me often and told me I was a 'gold star' worker. He'd also state how beautiful I was and ask me to marry him on a regular basis. I was only sixteen.

Initially I thought he was joking, but time would prove otherwise. I was asked to do morning shifts one week, and he offered to pick me up from my house each morning. I agreed, and one morning he started lingering over me in his van as he sniffed my neck. He said, 'You smell like a baked dinner.' I felt incredibly uncomfortable.

These occurrences, plus my feelings for Mary, were becoming too overwhelming, so I quit abruptly. I had an absolute meltdown and cut off all my hair!

A couple of weeks later, the husband showed up at my house. He begged me to come back and work for him again. I guess you could say he gaslighted me because I caved and agreed to come back.

The following week, I went back to work. I remember Mary's initial reaction to my new hairdo. She said, 'You look older with short hair', then smiled. I melted. I thought to myself, 'Perhaps she'll like me now.' But no, I was left disappointed.

As the weeks passed, I dropped the ball in terms of my work performance. I had nothing left to give. It all got too much, so yet again I broke down. I ended up in tears at the shop and the husband pulled me aside for a chat. He asked, 'What is going on with you, Saffire?' He then proceeded to tell me, 'Your baby tears aren't going to work this time.'

I didn't understand why he appeared to hate me. I mean, why did he assume that I was deliberately crying? I just wanted everything to go back to normal. He spoke to me as if there was a secret language, something going on between us. Once he realised I wasn't catching on, he got frustrated and told me, 'Snap out of it, and get back to work.'

I felt so small and confused by what was happening. I couldn't do it anymore, so I walked back into the shop and asked Mary if I could leave. She replied with no empathy, 'You can leave.' That broke me. Coming from her, I expected a better response.

I recall hearing a few weeks later that two of the girls I'd trained and befriended left not long after me. They didn't want to work there anymore if I wasn't there. I found that quite flattering. They remembered the true version of me – before the husband started tainting my name and badmouthing me to all the regulars and everyone in the shopping centre, saying I'd left his business in the lurch. In hindsight, if I knew what I know now, I'd put him in his place.

All I can say is thank goodness that more people are finally starting to speak up about these kind of transgressions … especially in relation to the 'Me Too' movement! It just makes you wonder – how many stories are out there that are similar to mine? I feel great empathy for the people who've experienced far worse! I mean, that's some kick-arse adversity right there! Needless to say that business failed for many factors, and the shop was sold yet again.

During this time I was unemployed for a short while on my quest to seek a better job, whilst neglecting to address the trauma that I'd just experienced.

I had my first experience with alcohol at the age of seventeen. Mum rarely drank, but she happened to buy a cask of wine on one particular occasion. I remember taking sneaky sips from the cask whenever she wasn't looking. I got very drunk, then proceeded to cry my eyes out as I confessed of my feelings for Mary to Mum. Mum had already suspected that I liked girls and took it rather well. (I was one of the lucky ones in this department. Sadly, other people aren't so fortunate.)

The following morning I woke up to my very first and worst hangover . I avoided alcohol for two years after that.

At this stage of my development I identified as bisexual in order to give myself room for exploration regarding my true preference.

For a brief moment in time our neighbourhood experienced some much needed peace. A few of the original neighbours moved out and were replaced with quieter people.

To my disappointment, one of the neighbours who left was Sam. I was shattered. Granted we had drifted apart, but there was an overwhelming feeling of being left behind. Everyone else was moving on and I was stuck in the very neighbourhood that had tormented me for years.

The peace was short lived, though, and a year later chaos erupted in our street yet again. We began to witness a new era of people moving in, with a middle-aged woman (who also identified as bisexual), along with her straight male ex, moving in to Sam's old house next door. Prior to my awareness of her orientation, I openly told her that I like girls. I was lonely and vulnerable, and I had no friends to share this information with in order to help decipher my thoughts and feelings.

Not long after this discussion I was invited into her home as she wanted to 'show me something' upstairs. As I followed her upstairs I found myself reminiscing over all the times I'd shared with Sam in this very house, and felt a sadness come over me. The lady walked me into her bedroom and gave me a look that alluded to her having an ulterior motive. My gut dropped, and I immediately recognised that something was up! I thought to myself, 'Oh crap, you're expecting us to have sex.' I quickly made an excuse to leave. It's safe to say I never associated with her again!

I denied my sexuality based on this experience for many years, as it caused me to associate bisexuality with something sleazy and gross.

That very year, I started a job as a cashier at McDonald's in Tumbi Umbi. The same week I started my new job, a neighbourhood disturbance broke out on the street.

It was my day off. This particular neighbour had recently lost his mother and had endured a nervous breakdown. He was yelling out, 'I'm going to kill everyone in the street.'

I recall peering out of my bedroom window overlooking the street as it all transpired. I froze as a flash of childhood memories came flooding in and I stood in terror as he grabbed an axe and charged toward townhouse number eighteen where an old lady lived. He then proceeded to smash her window open and attempted to enter the premises to kill her. I unfroze then ran downstairs to call the police, though it appeared that someone had already beaten me to the punch, because the police arrived and quickly arrested him.

I was traumatised beyond capacity, and begged Mum to request a housing transfer. Enough was enough! A woman came to our house to interview us regarding our reasons for seeking a transfer. For some reason I found myself having to do most of the talking, as Mum was quiet regarding the subject, and told the lady of the countless disturbances that had compromised our safety over the years.

'I'll see what I can do,' she said.

'You won't do anything,' I responded. 'You wouldn't understand, you don't know what it's like to live in a place like this.'

She replied, 'Yes, I do.' She left, and a week later she found us a place.

It's amazing just how quickly an assumption can be made based on a first impression – then can lead to a re-evaluation of a person based on a few words in a matter of seconds. We don't always know someone's story until we know it.

The new house was in Watanobbi on the Central Coast of NSW. I recall the day that we moved. It was an emotional experience. I cried so much, though it was a cry of relief.

The next-door neighbours on our right were a loud, large family, with a mother, a father, two teenage boys, a teenage girl and other family members who visited them on a daily basis. The neighbours to our left were middle-aged and more traditional.

As Mum and I walked down the driveway of our new home, our neighbours peered down at us from their balcony.

The boys had an uneasy smile as they said, 'Hey.'

I replied, 'Hello,' yet remained reserved.

The boys exuded a very intimidating and rough demeanour. I thought to myself, 'Oh no, not again.' The last thing Mum and I needed was more trouble.

Chapter 4

Identity Crisis

Mum and I befriended the neighbours to our left and we became quite close with the lady. Her name was Beth. We'd finally found a decent neighbour! Beth was an absolute treasure and brought Mum and I so much happiness. Sadly, she passed away a year later. It would be my first experience of grief.

I decided to transfer to a McDonalds that was closer to home, so transferred to Westfield Tuggerah. I made friends with the Head Chef. He was thirty years old and quickly expressed his interest in me. Needless to say I was flattered, as I rarely received attention from guys. He asked me out on a date and, even though I wasn't attracted to him, he appeared safe so I agreed.

We went out to dinner. Nineteen year old me was fresh to the world of dating. I ordered soup because I was too scared to eat in front of him. I'd never been that close to a guy before in such an intimate setting. I barely touched my soup and I didn't know how to communicate. I felt so uncomfortable, yet found myself agreeing to hang out with him again. What can I say, I liked the company. I mean, I literally had no friends and I was lonely.

On the second date, he started to hint at his desire to kiss me. I couldn't bring myself to do it. I avoided it for as long as I could, then the inevitable time drew nearer – I had to honour my true feelings and tell him that I didn't feel compatible with him. I was as nice as possible, but it didn't go down so well. Thankfully he got over it and started dating another girl.

All I craved was a woman's soft lips and feminine touch. It was excruciating. Puberty had finally hit, and I couldn't even act on it. I wasn't ready to face my true feelings, and there was no support in the community to help me understand what was happening to me.

I decided to leave McDonalds to look for a job that was more aligned with the direction of where I was going. The only issue was I didn't know what direction that was. As I look back, I was the kind of person who'd just take whatever opportunity that was presented and trial it until I failed. I never thought about my personal interests or options.

I was unemployed for about a year. I guess I was trying to figure it all out. During this time I became depressed and started comfort-eating and drinking alcohol on weekends with Mum, though Mum would only end up having a modest two beverages. I gained a lot of weight and it impacted my confidence (as weight gain generally does). I went from a size 8 to a size 16.

I spent most of my teens in solitude without any friends. I'd peer out of my window just longing for answers. Nothing made sense.

Suddenly, on my way to catch a bus to do Mum's weekly shopping, a girl around my age asked me when the next bus was due to arrive. I responded, 'I don't know.' Despite my abrupt dismissal, the girl remained polite and we both boarded the bus. I always chose to sit at the back of the bus as it felt safer. I recall her looking back at me with these beautiful blue eyes as she smiled. (I didn't know that I was attracted to her). So what did I do? I looked away.

Anyway, a week later I walked up the road to the local supermarket and I noticed a girl stepping out of the hairdressers. She was waving at me and smiling … it was her! What did I do? I looked right through her and walked on by. As I walked away, I couldn't help but look back at her. I saw her take a step back in sheer embarrassment and she looked the other way. I was kicking myself.

I was very attracted to her, but I felt so dirty. All I could think of was that fifty-year-old lady from my previous neighbourhood who'd made a move on me, and it made me feel gross. I didn't want to like girls!

I attempted to go on a date with another guy, but it didn't feel natural. When I returned home, I walked inside and gave Mum a look of defeat. I was twenty years old and I'd never been kissed!

To make matters worse, my adopted grandfather was present during this time, and he suggested buying me a cheap car. It was the biggest thing that had ever happened to me and I was grateful! Sadly, my excitement was overshadowed when he became a little too touchy-feely with me. As his hand slid across my chest in a sexually suggestive manner, I knew there was more to his kind proposition than was initially anticipated.

He'd once had intimate relations with my mother long before I was ever conceived. So from my Mum's perspective, the idea that he was expressing his interest in me thirty years later was just dead-set gross! I mean, he was in his eighties! I struggled to comprehend the reason as to why you'd think it was okay to hit on someone so young, not to mention someone who'd thought of you as their grandfather. He also knew about the sexual harassment that I endured as a sixteen year old and how that had impacted me. How did the lines get blurred?

When I attempted to confront and address the issue, he deflected and expressed his disappointment in me. Needless to say, we never spoke again.

So Mum and I were alone again. But hey, we had a car to get us from A to B. Life was good, right? This would solve all our problems. Ha… don't get me wrong, I was grateful. But that car didn't last any longer than a year, and the consequences behind receiving it left a lasting mark. I sold it for $600 to a local dealer.

As the year passed, I became more and more wary of our neighbourhood. I recall two men following me home one day in a white vehicle. They followed me all the way to my driveway with sinister expressions on their faces. I wasn't nervous about them doing anything during the daytime. I was more concerned about their intentions during the night-time. I decided to approach the car with my phone and proceeded to take photos of their licence plate and of their faces. They quickly drove off and never returned. Regardless, I grew scared of men as they made me feel as though I were under threat, having grown up with stories that men would rape and harm you.

A week later, the neighbours to our right had a massive party and drunkenly hung used condoms on our clothing line. We didn't address it in order to keep the peace.

During this period, Mum and I got a computer and connected to the wonderful world of social media. Good old MySpace! This is where it all went pear shaped – social media can be a dangerous tool for navigating relationships, as it's a lot easier to let loose and be braver.

I got a job at a bakery and I was finally eligible for a credit card. I'd also recently dyed my hair blonde, got a fake tan, bought the latest fashion trends and I'd lost a lot of weight. I looked like your typical blonde bombshell. It was an expensive process that left me $10,000 in debt. I became bankrupt as a result of keeping up appearances. When they say 'youth is wasted on the young,' they're not wrong.

Around this stage of my development, I finally come to terms with my sexuality, or so I thought. I reached out to my old school friend Terrie and apologised for hurting her in our early teenage years. She forgave me and invited me to go clubbing with her and her friends. I was introduced to one of their guy friends – let's just say I confirmed my sexuality by dating him. I had so many people telling me that I should explore my options, so I did. He was a nice guy with highly attractive features, but the idea of kissing him repulsed me and I couldn't go any further with him in relation to intimacy.

I remember him driving me home from a weekend away and we were listening to Michelle Branch in the car. Her song 'Are You Happy Now?' was playing, and a tear came to my eye. Even though the context of the song was unrelated to what I was going through, the sentiment provided me with a revelation. I wasn't happy. In that very moment, I realised my true feelings toward women, and became painfully aware that I'd never be happy if I continued to deny my true identity.

I remember when I returned home from the weekend away, I cried on Mum's shoulder and told her, 'Mum, I'm gay.'

Mum replied, 'It's okay, I already knew.'

My decision to date this guy also caused bit of drama amongst Terrie's friends. Most of them turned on me and I received a lot of harsh messages. I apologised profusely, but hey, these things happen on the road to self-discovery. You make decisions that ultimately impact other people along the way and it's inevitable ... Otherwise, how does one grow? At least I uncovered my sexual identity!

Shortly after, I went to the local grocery store and happened to bump into the girl I'd been kicking myself over for the past year. During this time, I had no idea as to what kind of lesbian I identified as. This was a thing back then – you were either the boy of the relationship or the girl. I didn't know how she'd react to my feminine attributes, as I really wanted to impress her from a masculine perspective.

Needless to say, she didn't give me the time of day. Perhaps she was rightfully ignoring me after I'd ignored her, but no. To my sheer disappointment, she was pregnant and approaching her boyfriend! I felt like an utter douchebag for allowing myself to obsess over someone who was straight this entire time. Isn't it amazing – the illusions you can create in your mind without any warning.

I needed a life cleanse. I asked Mum if I could declutter the house and she agreed. I got rid of many of our possessions and most of my clothes. Little did I know, I was clearing the way in order to make space for new people and much needed change.

I initiated a friendship with a girl who worked at a butcher nearby ... well, if I'm honest, I asked her on a date. Instead, she kindly declined and invited me to hang out with her and her friends. They were all country bumpkins with a love of partying. I remember having so much fun with this group of people.

While hanging out with them occupied my weekends, my weekdays were unfulfilled and I was starting to become riddled with anxiety and panic attacks. Anxiety wasn't something that I understood during this time so I went to the doctor, who confirmed that I have an anxiety/panic disorder. The anxiety was a combination of various unresolved issues, including my childhood trauma, low sense of self-worth, abandonment issues, questioning my identity, where I was going in life, and my concerns regarding my mother's ill health.

I ended up on financial support which required me to seek permanent employment. I worked for the dole for a while, then took part in a job seekers workshop. From those classes, I scored myself a part-time role as a receptionist in a corporate environment.

On one particular night, Mum caught a bus with me and we ventured out to do some late-night shopping. I walked past a fish and chip shop and one of the female workers was staring at me. She looked like your stereotypical token lesbian. She was a real lesbian, in real life!

As I casually walked past her, this girl gave me 'the look'. I instantly knew that she was gay and I suspected that she was into me. I wasn't being delusional this time around … this was legitimate! So I wrote my name and number on a piece of paper, asking her on a date. I nervously approached her, quickly placed it on her work bench and abruptly power-walked away.

She sent me a text message ten minutes later expressing utter appreciation. She proceeded to tell me that she was indeed checking me out, but she was seeing someone. She did, however, set me up on a date with her ex instead, strangely enough. It was dead-set awkward because the fish and chip shop girl tagged along as well.

Nothing came of that experience, though it did inspire me to venture out into the lesbian club scene, as they advised me of a trendy gay bar that was located within reasonable distance of my neighbourhood. I thought to myself, 'How did I not know about this place!?' I was twenty-one years old and I was about to commence an interesting journey, to say the least.

Chapter 5

They Never Warn You

I remember walking into the club like a deer in the headlights. Everyone was looking at me as though I was fresh meat. I didn't know what to expect, though I felt elated. I mean, I was amongst my people. This made sense.

The lesbian scene was fast paced, and let's just say that getting dates was easy. People had a knack for finding you online after each club appearance.

An older woman named Andy approached me online and asked me to dinner. Andy was a forty-year-old chef, and she'd be my first experience in proper dating. I wasn't exactly attracted to her, though her confidence regarding her affection toward me made me feel rather special. It's amazing what the power of confidence can do – that's all a person needs in order to attain what they want.

Andy taught me a thing or two about boundaries. At first, she pulled out every flattering thing you could say to win my affections … but eventually I'd wake up to text messages out of nowhere through all hours of the night and into the early hours of the morning that indicated a need for control

– questions like, 'Where are you? Who are you with? What have I done?' Then she'd express outbursts of rage toward me.

I also introduced Andy to my mother – yet she displayed no respect toward her. This was a huge turn off for me. If you disrespect my mother, you disrespect me! Lastly, I discovered that Andy had a girlfriend in Queensland. I soon stopped seeing her.

So I went back out into the lesbian club scene and got bombarded with copious amounts of attention – surprisingly by people who'd previously rejected me. I won't lie, it was validating!

I started seeing a girl named Jessie. She loved all things Asian, and she was obsessed with Korean boy-bands. I was at a stage where I wanted to be in control, so I naively opted to be the boy within a lesbian dynamic. I guess I never wanted to be treated like I had been by someone like Andy ever again! Oh, was I about to learn a thing or two!

Jessie was very girly and initially she appeared quite sweet. I guess I didn't notice how controlling she was until the end. It turned out Jessie was somebody that required you to prove yourself to her. She made you work for it, so I did. I did everything I could possibly do to make her feel safe and valued. Even though I was recently unemployed I still made sure that I took the traditional approach, showering her with flowers and paying for her meals whenever we'd go out. Granted, I was still uncertain about what I wanted to do with my life, and as a consequence Jessie's mother didn't approve of me, as she wanted her daughter to date someone who had money. This I respected, but her approach toward me was indeed derogatory. Man, I really feel for men right now with what's expected of them from a traditional viewpoint.

Jessie would be my first sexual experience ... but the only time I felt good enough for her was during intimacy, because that was the only time she'd praise me. Other than that, Jessie sided with her mother regarding our issues. I felt utterly worthless. Whenever I got sick she was never there for me like I was for her. Whenever we fought, she'd always highlight the areas in which she believed I lacked and I'd always end up being the one trying to make amends, even if I wasn't at fault.

It got worse. She started premeditating situations where she knew I'd catch a glimpse of her phone when she'd been sending flirty messages to others. Her phone would be strategically placed on her bed, intentionally unattended with an open message ... she was no fool!

One time I recall her altering my picture with Photoshop by replacing my brown eyes with blue eyes. Then there were other times she'd calculate the exact moment that I was about to walk into her room so that I'd catch her peering longingly at pictures of her ex-girlfriend.

She kept me on my toes mentally and emotionally, and it was taking its toll on my self-esteem. Everyone in Jessie's circle believed I wasn't good enough for her.

I don't want to end this chapter, or any other of my chapters for that matter, as though I'm intending to throw anyone under the bus. My intention is simply to demonstrate the behaviours within a relationship that can inevitably impact a person on their road toward self-discovery, especially in a world full of careless destruction, manipulation, and misconduct.

It's so easy to persecute and judge someone like myself from an outsider's perspective. I didn't have money, I was uneducated and I had no direction in life. I was therefore considered a lost cause in the eyes of others.

I don't know why, but people often neglect to remember that we make poor choices in our youth based on naivety. How is anyone expected to make sensible decisions when you haven't had a chance yet to discover who you truly are yet? Already somebody is trying to label you with their opinions of who they perceive you to be. Those negative opinions only confirm in our young and impressionable minds that we are indeed worthless – hence why so many people continue to fall into toxic relationships. You simply don't have a chance to discover your true potential unless somebody is kind enough to see past how society perceives you.

If you don't know who you are, or understand the necessity of knowing your worth (especially at such a young age), you're doomed to attract people who attempt to mould you into what they require you to be. It doesn't make the people who resort to these strategies bad people

– it's a psychological condition for those who feel worthless themselves. It's nothing personal, even though it may appear to be at times.

Some people resort to externalising those needs through 'romantic idealisms' – the things we 'want' rather than 'need' in a relationship. Those idealisms aren't a true reflection of what authentic love resembles, though, yet some people find momentary comfort within this concept. We set standards for ourselves, and some people just settle in fear of being alone or not being able to do better.

These types of individuals will target you if you haven't yet established who you are, as they want to 'create' you and take credit for your identity. Call it narcissism, but perhaps it's beyond that. Me? I call it survival, disguised as a false sense of security to avoid sitting in uncomfortable truths.

I now know that Jessie didn't feel like she was enough, so deflected the attention away from herself by making me question myself. Why? It was because she didn't want to lose me.

Ultimately the only thing separating me from what everyone wanted her to attain within the relationship was money. I had everything else going for me – I just didn't know it at the time.

When you have a team of people constantly supporting your worth (as Jessie's family and friends were) and the other person has no one in their corner (like me), it's easy for someone in Jessie's shoes to feel 'worthy' and have all the power. Jessie may not have had self-belief during this period – but the validation from her family and friends provided her with a sense of entitlement, as she had people defending her sense of value. You see, I didn't have that. So for someone in my shoes, one might succumb to their weaknesses and seek validation of their worth. You're made to believe that you have to prove your worth to the person questioning it. I like to see the good in people. If you give someone the power to control your emotions (and have little awareness of what you're feeling), then that person will use this to their advantage, with a negative impact on your wellbeing.

When we're young, we don't always have the internal resources or strength to be selfless and vulnerable in order for a relationship to be healthy and functional. It's human to react from fear, especially when you're in your twenties.

I digress. I'll end my point by stating that Jessie was enough.

I was enough.

We just weren't right for one another.

I forgive Jessie, even if she isn't sorry – because I know what it's like to react from a place of fear. Plus, in retrospect, she was just a kid.

I also forgive myself for my own shortcomings – because I, too, was just a kid.

Nevertheless, it was evident that my primary weakness going forward would be to seek the approval of others. In my young mind, if I couldn't sustain perfection, I simply wasn't enough.

Chapter 6

Learning The Hard Way

One night I recall going to the local pub as it was karaoke night. I sang 'Hollywood' by Madonna, and a local talent scout spotted me. He said, 'I want to introduce you to a band. Your voice would be perfect for them.' Although I was excited by the proposition, I failed to commit to the offer as I just wasn't ready.

That very month, Jessie went away to Wagga for the weekend alone, and I decided to occupy my time by heading out with some new people that I'd met online. I made friends with two girls in particular, Ally and Emma. To my surprise, they both expressed their interest in me half way through the night. One could say they'd had too much 'truth serum'. Ally was single and made it clear that she wanted me. Emma was taken, yet expressed a desire of a similar nature. I'll admit, all this attention was immediately gratifying, but my moral compass was screaming at me so I proceeded to speak to everyone in a platonic manner. I mean, I didn't know this was a thing – that people pursued people who were already seeing someone. I found it to be a very ballsy act … not in a good way!

Once the night had ended, Emma drunkenly gravitated toward me. I was rather drunk myself, whilst maintaining my resting bitch face because I didn't want to confuse the situation, and I never wanted to hurt Jessie. However, despite my best efforts to set boundaries between Emma and I, Emma told me that she had fallen for me. Sigh, young love. Then Emma tried to kiss me, but I declined – though if I'm truly honest, I wanted to kiss her. She made me feel like I was enough. I didn't have to prove myself to her.

The following day I told Jessie everything. As shocked as she was, she forgave me. I attempted to make it work for about a week in order to maintain the connection between Jessie and I … but eventually gave into my true feelings and pulled the plug. I had to do the right thing by everyone, including myself.

So Emma left her girlfriend, and I stopped dating Jessie. Needless to say, I quickly became the villain of the narrative between Jessie and I – and Jessie's family and friends felt my unworthiness had been confirmed.

Emma and I only hung out for about two weeks. Nothing serious happened – but I was grateful for meeting her, as she was the catalyst for escaping my turbulent connection with Jessie. Meanwhile, Jessie remained in my life as a friend. I guess she was hanging onto hope that I'd eventually go back to her, despite my best efforts to encourage her otherwise.

About a month later – I hate to admit it, but I started dating my friend Ally, believing that she was the 'nice girl' that I should be dating. She appeared to be lovely initially, but I didn't feel that instant attraction as I had with Emma, and we didn't have as much of an intellectual connection. We were simply incompatible. It almost felt like I was talking to a brick wall ... but her affection toward me had a strong pull. She was good with flattering words, and as I felt so unworthy after my experience with Jessie I naturally gravitated toward any form of validation I could. Mind you, I wasn't aware of this pattern at the time. I was twenty-two years old.

During this time, Jessie begged me to go to Queensland with her for her birthday as we'd planned prior to our separation. Ally knew that there was nothing to worry about in regards to anything happening between Jessie and I – Ally knew that I'd eat my hat before I'd ever consider rekindling a connection like that. It was purely platonic! So with permission from Ally I decided to go, out of respect for Jessie.

Jessie and I flew to Queensland and we had a great time! We explored many theme parks and we stayed in a nice hotel. It was my first trip out of the state, and it was blissful. I enjoyed just having a friend (regardless of the fact that Jessie was an ex) and being far away from home.

I started to reflect on what I truly needed at this point in my life, and Ally wasn't a part of that vision. Time away from her made me realise just how wrong it all was. I guess I needed the space in order to see that. Perhaps this getaway was merely an excuse to reflect on all that had transpired. I mean, prior to the getaway, I started to notice Ally was a completely different person behind the scenes compared to the lovable character she portrayed to everyone she knew, and this raised a few concerns for me. Don't get me wrong, Ally wasn't a bad person – but she had a few character traits that I found to be insensitive. Granted I was and am a highly sensitive person, so the match was doomed to fail before it even began.

I was a size twelve at this stage, and in the lesbian scene this wasn't ideal as skinnier people were more favoured. Yeah, sad right? Ally would mock my weight by jiggling my hips whilst stating 'It's cute' in a derogatory manner. It made me feel unattractive. Whenever I had no make-up on, she'd make it known just how unappealing I looked in my natural state. She'd also speak to me with a condescending tone whenever I spoke of anything remotely profound.

I stopped seeing Ally when I returned home from the getaway. We stayed friends and she started to see other people. I attempted to spend a short period of my life in solitude in order to figure my crap out, though it didn't last long, as I disliked my own company. I ended up going on a few dates with various individuals, though nobody appealed to me on an emotional level. With every encounter, something wasn't quite right. As a result of this, despite the fact that I never slept with anyone I got labelled a player. I guess I unintentionally hurt a few people.

One night I saw Ally at our local gay club. Something strange came over me when I noticed Ally flirting with other girls. I felt jealous, but why? I didn't know what I was feeling, so I presumed it was love. I pondered this for a few days and eventually I messaged her stating how much I missed her. She responded, 'I miss you, too.' That message wasn't enough for me, though. I wanted her back, despite how incompatible we were. So I asked her if she'd be willing to give it another go. What happens next is ultimately on me. She contemplated this for a couple of days, then she replied, 'yes.'

I decided to tell Jessie my decision. Jessie was naturally furious with me, as she genuinely thought I'd go back to her. And Ally requested that I no longer have contact with Jessie, which was merited – so I complied.

I attempted to get to know Ally's family, but in all honesty nobody liked me. They all believed that I was a drop-kick and that Ally could do better. History has a funny way of repeating itself, doesn't it?

In order to add fuel to the fire, a nice little rumour circulated through the community that Jessie and I had been seen kissing on the dance floor at the local gay bar on a night that Ally was away – an event that was positioned right under a security camera, and could be reviewed in a matter of minutes through proper investigation. I suggested that my innocence could be proven through this method, but nobody budged. No matter what I said, I remained a villain. I learned that if people don't like you, they're committed to their dislike of you whether it's merited or not. This hurt me for quite some time, and I was interrogated about this rumour for many years to follow.

The truth? This rumour came about as a result of a date I'd been on with a girl prior to my reconciliation with Ally – a girl I'd rejected who'd decided to seek revenge. This girl was pals with one of Ally's friends, so therefore Ally's friend defended her, leaving me with no allies. Needless to say, it caused some issues between Ally and I. I'd spend months proving myself to her because she kept getting swept up in the stories that circulated around the town. It was exhausting. The one thing that hurt me most of all was being accused of something that I didn't do. I was a good partner.

As the months passed I started to believe that perhaps Ally was the one – so I pulled a stupid and asked her to marry me. I drove her to a beach and replicated a scene from the movie *Love Actually*, entailing cards asking her to be my wife. Granted it wouldn't be a real wedding (due to the Australian laws back then), but it would be a modest and heartfelt commitment ceremony. I wanted to show her that I was legitimate.

By this stage Ally's mum had her own doubts about me. Ally's mum believed the rumours and proceeded to try and warn her daughter against me, which was fair enough.

Sometimes I wish a lie detector test had been suggested because I would've passed with flying colours.

Prior to the ceremony, I started to lose a substantial amount of weight. I went from 64 kilos to 52 kilos in a matter of two months. I practically starved myself – I wanted to feel like I was enough, in all regards. I guess I associated my weight as a representation of my sense of self-worth. The one thing that confused me the most during this time was having people comment on how amazing I looked. It only exacerbated my cravings in order to feel accepted.

Anyway, I started working at a chicken shop, and on one of my days off I noticed that Ally left her phone unattended. I happened to pick up her phone out of curiosity and had a sneaky peek at her text messages. Ally had started flirting online with a girl from New Zealand.

The following day, Ally walked past my place of work and noticed that I couldn't even look at her. She attempted to rectify the situation and I instantly forgave her … but in all honesty, I had my suspicions from that point onwards that she wasn't entirely happy with me if she was looking elsewhere. Something shifted within me, and my loyalty and devotion was less apparent. I'll admit, I was no saint. When Ally and I went out for drinks to our local gay bar, I got drunk and danced suggestively with other girls. Granted, they were just friends, but the tone was inappropriate. It would appear that I, too, had a wandering eye, but I never acted on it any further.

It was quite evident that we weren't ready to make a commitment to one another, but Ally and I proceeded to have the commitment ceremony nevertheless. In every photo Ally appeared to be embarrassed, like she was making the biggest mistake of her life — which I understand now, in hindsight.

Two months later, Ally left me for a sixteen year old she'd met at work. Initially, I felt like I was going crazy because my instincts were telling me that something was going on between them, yet I was being told something of an entirely different nature. 'Oh no, we're just friends, promise.' Once I witnessed cryptic content on the other girl's social media account, I decided to put my foot down. I put a stop to their friendship, only to discover that they were already hanging out behind my back. I'll never forget the moment I caught them. Ally said, 'She just makes me smile' with a sinister smile upon her face, as if she wanted to hurt me.

The day Ally decided to 'fess up and tell me the truth about her feelings, I was driving her to work. She said, 'I think I've liked her for a while, I just couldn't admit it to myself'. My gut sank and I almost slammed on the breaks.

I approached the other girl after Ally finished work. I tried to remain calm to ask her what was going on. The other girl displayed no remorse, as if she didn't have to justify herself to me. I guess you could say that the other girl, and her lack of care-factor, inflamed my ego and I reacted. As I walked away from her, I grabbed Ally's hand and we walked to the car. I wanted to appear like I still had some control over the situation. My entire body felt like it had been poisoned ... I'd never experienced such adrenaline in my entire life. I recall swallowing my pride as I got down on my knees in the car park and I begged Ally to choose me. (Of course this would have gratified her ego beyond capacity). Ally swiftly declined.

Despite the fact that I wasn't the cause of our breakup, Ally's family and friends proceeded to congratulate her for exiting a toxic relationship and for choosing a better option. Ha, no words are needed here. Ally remained with this girl for three years – then, out of nowhere she messaged me, stating her regret. Deep down, I knew that she was only messaging me because the other girl had done the dirty on her – and now Ally was now in the same position that I was in three years ago. I agreed to meet up with her in order to gain some closure in my attempt to be evolved. We both tried to rekindle our friendship, but it became very apparent that we weren't compatible, even as friends.

I did struggle with this chapter for quite some time prior to completing this book. I experienced a lot of anger and I found it hard to trust people. I remained quite adamant that I wasn't enough for many years based on these events.

But I was enough.

Ally was enough.

We just weren't right for each other ... and that's okay!

I didn't deserve what happened to me – but it's about what you learn on the journey toward self-discovery. You won't become aware of who you are without the impact of negative experiences. It's inevitable.

I forgive Ally, even if she isn't sorry ... she was just a kid.

I also forgive myself for my own shortcomings.

Chapter 7

A Downward Spiral

What does one do after enduring such betrayal? One goes on a date, and the cycle continues!

I met a girl named Soozie. We'd been speaking online for a short while and she made me feel special. (Those damn feelings get me into trouble every time). Soozie was an alpha female who worked as a corporate in the outskirts of the city. She'd had her fair share of fun in the lesbian scene and she had her sights set on me.

I recall the first night that we hung out. We went to a lesbian nightclub in the city. Soozie marked her territory with an overly confident demeanour. Nobody was to get in her way. It was almost predatory as I reflect back. I remember being caught off guard as she kissed me without warning. I found it to be a massive turn-off, though I proceeded to go along with it as I hadn't learned how to set boundaries at that stage.

It was arranged that Soozie and I would stay at her friend's house that night. The only option was the couch, though, so we shared it. As we sat on the couch Soozie pulled me into her, then started to kiss me. She proceeded to state just how badly she wanted to have sex with me, but I told her that I didn't sleep with people on the first night. Soozie dismissed what I said and continued to kiss me. I felt so uncomfortable – nothing about this situation was appealing to me, yet she continued to hint at her desire to have sex with me. This should have been my first red flag, but I was alone and desperate for company. I almost felt guilty for not going through with anything. If I'm brutally honest, I just wanted a friend.

The following day when I returned home, I messaged Soozie and told her that I just wanted to be her friend. She couldn't accept this, so she called me incessantly and attempted to challenge my feelings and question my character for not being attracted to her.

With her consistent pursuit, I caved and went on another date with her. The more time we spent together, though, the more I found I liked her as a friend. She was a smart young woman and I really enjoyed her company. I didn't want to lose her, but at the same time I didn't want to commit to her. I merely wanted her friendship.

As I started to allow myself to set boundaries, I'd tell her, 'I'm single to the full extent' – but the higher I set my walls, the more controlling she became and the more confused I grew as a result. Within the space of two weeks, I chose to be intimate with her – and this only caused more issues. Whenever she tried to be intimate with me, she'd get frustrated by my fear of penetration, and by how long I took to orgasm externally. Everything felt so pressured.

Soozie would demonstrate her serious intentions towards me by visiting my mother on a regular basis – making me feel rather trapped. I felt like she'd only see my mum to make herself look good, so I appeared to be the ungrateful one.

I found myself becoming quite irritable when speaking to my mother. I guess I felt somewhat embarrassed by my home life. This embarrassment stemmed from witnessing how functional and normal Soozie's family was. Soozie's parents were separated, but they'd still attend family gatherings with utter grace and respect towards each other. Her family also had money and status. I felt like such an outsider whenever I attended social events with her. I felt so judged and compared.

Nevertheless, I appreciated Soozie for trying to show interest in my home life. She had some good qualities, I'll give her that. She even helped find me a job. I ended up getting Soozie's old job as she transferred into a new role. I absolutely sucked at administration, so it's safe to say I only got that gig thanks to her.

As the months passed, Soozie started to display some intense aggravation toward me. She couldn't just let me be me, and she was adamant to claim me as her own!

I recall some horrific fights. At the time I was staying with Soozie and her dad – and when things got overly heated, I'd pack my bag in an attempt to leave the house. Soozie would pin me down onto the bed as she proceeded to yell at me. Other times, Soozie would block me from exiting the main door. Then she'd pin me against the wall as she punched it a centimetre away from my face.

One night she put both of her hands around my throat and said, 'You f**king c**t, you f**king dumb bitch' – like she wanted to squeeze the life out of me.

She would go into an absolute rage if I stood up for myself. It became pretty evident that we brought out the worst in each other. One night I smashed her blender on the kitchen floor. I'd had enough of being told who I could hang out with and what I should or shouldn't be doing. I felt horrible, and I replaced her blender the following day.

These incidents took place whenever we'd discuss my need for freedom. I kept reinforcing the fact that I was too damaged and that I wasn't ready to be in another relationship. I tried to warn her on a continuous basis. I needed to figure out who I was, but her patience was running out. I knew that I'd lose her forever if I didn't commit to her.

I remember one night on our bus ride home from nightclubbing, Soozie said with a look of defeat, 'My friends were right, you're never going to be with me. I give up.' With fears that I'd lose her forever and that I'd be going back home alone again, I promptly made my decision. I bought her a red rose and I asked her to be my girlfriend.

Don't get me wrong, I loved Soozie! She had so much to offer someone, but her control mechanisms and inability to just let me be me made it difficult for me to trust or feel safe with her. As the weeks passed, I really struggled to be with her. I declared that I wanted to stop dating on many occasions, and told her I just wanted to be friends. She never listened and acted as if I was her property. She'd watch me like a hawk, and I was never allowed to think my own thoughts or feel my own emotions. I didn't know it back then, but she was grooming me.

We made the foolish decision to move out and into our own apartment in Sydney that we could hardly afford. I was about to study Audio Engineering & Sound Production at a music institute, and Soozie had scored herself a new job. From this point, I spiralled into a childlike state and Soozie became my lifeline. So much fear and anxiety overcame me … I couldn't do anything by myself. I was worried that Soozie would meet someone new at work and I was apprehensive about enduring the education system all over again.

Soozie's aggression toward me escalated. She started throwing me around the lounge room as if I were a ragdoll, leaving me with bruises trailing down my arms and legs. One night, I screamed so loud that the neighbours called the police. When the police arrived, Soozie retreated and displayed utmost remorse.

One of the police women looked at my arms and said, 'I can see the difference between fresh bruises and old bruises.' They could tell it was an ongoing thing. They gave Soozie a stern warning and told me to contact them if I experienced more trouble.

It all got the better of me and I started resorting to some bad habits. I just wanted to escape. I would day-drink, I became addicted to laxatives in order to manage my weight, and I took prescription medication in order to sleep. I felt like I was going insane – not to mention I was experiencing night terrors of being raped. To add fuel to the fire, Mum and I were fighting non-stop via text messages.

The one thing that brought me some hope was the music institute.

It wasn't too long until the worst of me took over, and I resorted to an unorthodox method in order to gain some power within my relationship. I wanted Soozie to experience what it felt like be me – to demonstrate to an abuser just how it feels to have your power stripped from you. I bought her a bunch of junk food and demanded that she eat it, threatening to leave her if she didn't. I knew that weight gain was her biggest weakness. It's all I could think of – I knew that it wouldn't cause her any physical or mental harm. I mean, it was only weight gain and she'd lose it rather quickly. Plus, the upside would be she'd enjoy her favourite treats in the process.

Regardless, I felt a lot of shame for using this method of approach. I wasn't proud of this behaviour and I punished myself for years.

Needless to say, all of Soozie's friends hated me and advised her against me. Two girls in particular would be the catalyst to us breaking up, which, in hindsight, I'm grateful for. Soozie started hanging out with some old friends she'd once had relations with. She'd get away with it because they were friends. I knew that I was losing her.

I recall her last birthday that I spent with her. Her friends remarked on how happy she looked because she was surrounded by her old crew. They proceeded to comment on how long it'd been since they'd seen her smile. These remarks were awfully familiar to comments that echoed from my past. I couldn't help but feel like the loser in our relationship. These incidents impeded my confidence and I started to feel unworthy of her – or of anyone, for that matter. I thought to myself, *It must be me, right?*

The final straw was receiving a text message from one of Soozie's friends, saying, 'Stay out of our friendship and we'll all be fine' – as if my existence in Soozie's life was irrelevant.

It was time. I decided to pack my bags and grab a train back home to the Central Coast. Soozie didn't put up a fight. She let me go. I missed and loved her when I left, but I knew I had to leave.

Just weeks after the breakup, I found out from one of Soozie's exes that she, too, had experienced physical and emotional abuse during their relationship. Her ex literally recited every word of what I'd experienced myself.

I'll end this chapter by saying that Soozie was a good person with wonderful qualities. She just didn't believe in herself and attempted to force a connection in order to validate her sense of self-worth. So she resorted to unhealthy patterns in order to manage these feelings of worthlessness.

Soozie was enough.

I was enough.

We just weren't right for one another, and that's okay.

Our behaviour toward each other wasn't acceptable, though. I don't condone any form of abuse. I'm simply expressing my compassion toward why a person may resort to this method of approach.

I forgive Soozie … I also forgive myself for my own shortcomings.

Chapter 8

Awakening

I won't lie. It was difficult living back at home again initially. It felt like I'd gone backwards. Little did I know that I needed to go backwards in order to go forward. After a month, I moved to the city to be closer to the music institute and jumped from sharehouse to sharehouse. It never lasted, though, and I'd find myself moving back home again. I couldn't catch a break.

I was carrying so much guilt regarding all that had transpired. I felt like I deserved my suffering, which ultimately caused me to attract the worst. I had no friends in order to lift my spirits during this time period, so Mum would be my only source of support, which in hindsight I see was a very positive thing.

It took some time for Soozie to contact me. She asked to see me but I declined. Instead I apologised for my role in our relationship breakdown, and she replied with remorse of a similar nature. She also added, 'Let me know when your mum dies. I really liked her.' I suspect she was attempting to instil fear into me in order to change my mind in regards to leaving her, because she knew that I'd be alone.

Soozie would resurface on numerous occasions throughout this period with questions as to why it didn't work out between us. I could tell that she was struggling to move forward. Heck, so was I. Eventually she met a really nice girl who truly loved her. Instead of acting out of pride, I told her to explore it. Even though I missed having her in my life, I had to do the right thing. I set us free.

Not long after our moment of closure, I did some soul-searching. I wanted to rectify all the damage that I may've caused others from my past, so I messaged every single person I'd ever gone on a date with or done wrong by, including all my exes. I provided everyone with a very lengthy message listing the areas in which I could've displayed better form. Most responses were lovely ... some, not so much. But hey, you can't please everyone.

On a completely unrelated topic – one day I felt compelled to record a video of myself singing, then I uploaded it to one of my social media accounts.

I was still attending the music institute around this time, which required long train rides to and from the city. My lecturer from class happened to come across my video and said that I had talent. He proceeded to suggest that I should start writing my own songs, so I decided to turn some of my old poems into lyrics and create a melody with some simple chords on my portable Casio piano.

Not long afterward I ventured out into the city to perform my newly written songs at a bunch of Open Mic nights. I would wander the city like a lost soul on a quest to find love and meaning in this life. I remember disguising a lot of tears behind my sunglasses on the train rides. My heart was aching, and music was my release.

I recall my first performance was to an audience of two people, and during another performance a man stood up and said, 'Get off the f**ken stage you f**ken c**t, you're shit.' But I carried on with my performance.

At times the conditions I travelled in were horrific. Let's just say that I was very brave for walking home from the train station so late at night.

During this period there were a lot of disturbances in our street. I recall feeling very triggered and my hypersensitivity to sound kicked in. Some nights I'd be trembling with fear for no apparent reason. It was like being a child again, but as an adult.

Something good transpired, though, and I happened to make a new friend online. Her name was Sharon and she lived in Melbourne. We became very good friends thanks to some in-depth phone calls and I'd eventually step outside of my comfort zone by travelling to Melbourne to see her. We were experiencing similar adversities and we'd become each other's rock for a while, before beginning to explore our friendship romantically. Let's just say that we shouldn't have gone there as it ruined a good thing. But our friendship did last for a couple of years.

I went on many dates through this period, and one in particular turned my world upside down.

Her name was Ebony. I met her at a gay church (don't ask haha). She looked like an angel, and I genuinely thought she was the one until I became painfully aware that I'd got myself into another situation where someone wanted to change me. She'd ridicule me for being unemployed and made derogatory comments about my life choices. This truly broke me, as I didn't spot the signs for several weeks. I'd deluded myself into believing that she was 'my person' because all I saw was magic.

I now see in hindsight that she was never going to commit to me as she wanted somebody who had their own home and drive in relation to their career. She didn't take my music seriously as it provided no financial source of income, which was fair enough. But she was hurtful in the way she expressed this – so I pulled the plug.

Mum and Sharon were both my rocks during this time. Going back home was a blessing in a lot of ways. I listened to Mum's stories all over again, but from a different viewpoint – this time with more of an open mind as I had a bit more life experience. Mum and I cried on each other's shoulders a lot, and we experienced some remarkable moments of healing together. Together we would have *Sex and the City* marathons and grab a coffee from our local convenience store every morning, while having in-depth discussions about life. We were best friends.

I decided to step up regarding my music. I recorded my songs into demos, I scored myself some paid gigs and had one of my tunes played on internet radio.

I also attempted to be more social, but was sexually harassed at a birthday party I attended, which turned me off going out for a while.

I also got to know the neighbour to our left a bit better. I'd sometimes go and have a few drinks with him on a Friday night to keep him company because he was alone. He died unexpectedly. As I was the only person who'd visited him, I became a suspect when all his belongings vanished from his house. His son and wife practically threatened me at my front door. I felt petrified, and I remember my mum being riddled with anger as she defended me. I was more concerned about my mum potentially having a heart attack. This occurrence had me on edge for a few days until Sharon decided to call my local police station and ask them a few questions to put my mind at rest. Thankfully, I wasn't in question and the threats proved to be false.

Later that year, I happened to see Soozie and her new lover walk past one of the venues that I played at. They looked grossly happy and in love. My gut sank. I had never felt more alone than I did in that moment. I knew I'd done the right thing, but I felt such a loss. I questioned why I hadn't found my 'one'. I thought to myself – perhaps it *was* me? Perhaps I brought out the worst in her because I *was* worthless? This wasn't the case, though – my life was just forming a different pattern to help me benefit long-term. Little did I know that I was on a journey of accepting myself, and believe me, in a world where everyone has different values, it's hard to be yourself and embrace your authenticity. But I was on my way to self-love and self-acceptance.

My dating life continued – and boom, I met Emily online. She was an eccentric 40-year-old business woman who lived in Brisbane. She had an intensity about her that appealed to me, and she wore her heart on her sleeve.

Emily decided to come to Sydney for a business trip and she wanted to meet me, so she invited me to spend the night with her in her hotel room. The night I spent with her was lovely, and we developed feelings for each other quite fast.

When Emily left Sydney, I couldn't wait to be with her again so we arranged to spend Valentines Day with each other. Emily bought me a train ticket to Brisbane for four days.

During the week prior to leaving for Brisbane, Mum was acting a little strange and wasn't 100 per cent herself. I recall her telling me, 'I'm glad you have Emily now, because I know she'd be there for you if anything happened to me.' I never thought anything of that comment at the time.

The day I left for Brisbane, I did Mum's shopping and paid her bills. We enjoyed a nice coffee together and she appeared to be very happy. Before I left, I gave her a massive cuddle that I can still feel to this very day.

I left for the train station and called Emily. Emily appeared defensive and proceeded to suggest I had no intention of coming to Brisbane. In utter confusion, I said, 'I'm at the train station with my bags.' She continued to speak to me in a defensive manner as if she didn't trust me.

I was starting to detect some red flags because Emily kept having these moments out of nowhere. One moment everything was great, and the next everything was sufficiently awkward. I felt so uncomfortable. A part of me just wanted to run away – but my gut told me to get on that train, so I did. Once I confirmed that I was on the train, Emily settled and reverted back to her loving self.

Forty minutes later Mum sent me a thesis-length message detailing how thankful she was for all the help I'd given her over the years. She also stated that I'd healed her, and that I'd eventually make it in music one day. It was strange, but I didn't think anything of it. I responded with utmost gratitude for the compliments.

Upon my arrival to Brisbane, Mum messaged me again to ask if I'd arrived safely. I assured her that I had, and Mum responded, 'Thank you, now I can sleep peacefully.'

During the day, I noticed Mum wasn't responding to any of my messages. It was unlike her. I had this gut feeling that something was up.

I had no one to contact in order to check on her, so I called the police and asked if they could knock on her door to see if she was okay.

An hour later, a policeman called me informing me of my mother's death.

Chapter 9

Losing Everything

I lost my mother and my best friend all at once. I was only twenty-nine years old.

Emily hugged me with tears in her eyes and said, 'I'm so sorry.' In utter shock I replied, 'It's okay, it's okay,' in my attempt to reassure her.

Emily took me to a bar and bought me a couple of drinks. When she went to the bathroom, I felt a hand upon on my knee, though nobody was present. I like to think that it was Mum and not just a random leg spasm.

Two hours later, I was questioned by police. I was a prime suspect for Mum's death because I was the only person in her life, and the coroner's report hadn't yet been established. I couldn't believe what was happening.

I woke up the following morning in hopes that it was all just a bad dream, but it wasn't. I remember curling up into a ball on Emily's bed and crying.

Emily took a week off work to accompany me back to Sydney, for which I was grateful. Prior to leaving Brisbane, Emily called her family and friends, telling me she needed to talk to them as this was hard for her, too. I totally respected it ... but the way in which she suggested it felt as though it was from a strange place.

Emily and I took turns at driving on our trip back to Sydney and I made all the calls that were necessary to handle Mum's affairs, including her cremation.

When we approached the driveway of my house, I remember seeing Irene, a new friend I'd made at an Open Mic night. She offered her assistance in helping me clean up the house before I returned the keys to the housing department.

I almost collapsed upon approaching the front door and I broke down into tears. I recall having two shots of vodka prior to entering the house. As I walked inside, the house wasn't the way I'd left it. The police had had to enter the premises via a window, and glass was everywhere. I'm just grateful they'd been the ones to discover her, not me – that image would've haunted me for life. I'll forever appreciate their services. In hindsight, I believe it was my intuition urging me to board the train to Brisbane so that I wouldn't witness the full extent of Mum's death.

As I walked upstairs and into Mum's bedroom, I saw an indentation in her bed from where she'd last slept.

Nevertheless, I pulled myself together in order to clean the house.

I told Irene that she could take anything that she wanted in appreciation for her help, so she took my brand new guitar and some of Mum's jewellery. There were also people walking into my mother's house from off the street like it was a garage sale. One woman went so far by attempting to steal my wallet. It was unreal. I make no judgment toward people who do what they need to do in order to survive – but hey, a woman had just died. I had five dollars to my name (prior to Mum's insurance money coming in), and I was already giving away all of the possessions Mum and I had accumulated over the years. Why go the extra mile?

Meanwhile, Emily was quite aloof towards me as we were cleaning the house. I found myself trying to comfort her out of consideration for her feelings. I was utterly confused. The only time that Emily would speak to me was if we were in the presence of Irene. It was just bizarre.

Amongst all the chaos, the funeral director swung by the house to obtain a signature for Mum's cremation. It was a hefty $4,000 bill. Mum's life insurance was $5,900. Thankfully I could cover it – though I didn't receive Mum's life insurance money until the following week. I was broke, so Mum's cremation was put on hold until then.

When we finished up for the day, Emily and I got in the car and she gave me a look that I knew wasn't good.

She said, 'Something isn't right here.' I asked her what she meant. Emily responded, 'I don't feel like you're being genuine with me.' She proceeded to suggest that I was cheating on her. I couldn't believe that this was happening. I mean, I was trying to hold my shit together so I wouldn't scare her away, and I'd just organised my mother's cremation. When would I have had the time to cheat on her?

We drove to a motel and Emily booked a room. The conversation continued for about an hour. Needless to say, I was very uncomfortable and distraught. I was sitting on the bed with tears in my eyes as she proceeded to interrogate me. She was cold and passive-aggressive, and I recall her smiling at one point of the discussion. I knew that she was intentionally trying to cause me distress.

It got to the point where I started to pack my bags and I was ready to leave. Even though I had nowhere to go to, I didn't care – my sanity was being compromised. I couldn't fathom how someone could do this to someone who had just lost a parent. I mean, who does that!? It was clear that she was trying to manipulate my vulnerability. Once Emily realised I wasn't going to allow myself to be subjected to her torment, she quickly apologised and proceeded to state that she was just scared because she was falling in love with me. I understand being scared, but really? This situation caused me to remain on edge, but I chose to forgive her and continued to ride the rollercoaster with her.

We planned to go back to Brisbane and it was agreed that I'd live with her. Once we settled back in Brisbane, I reached out to Sharon and Irene. Emily didn't like this, and further stated that she was concerned regarding their influence over me. I was only seeking their comfort in regards to my grief.

Things got worse. Most days Emily retreated without any warning. She continued to accuse me of being with her for the wrong reasons and proceeded to ask if I was cheating on her. She'd tell me, 'You're not giving me enough,' despite the fact that I was already suppressing my grief in order to constantly reassure her.

It got to the point where she started calling me 'fatty' once my appetite returned, and she called me shallow whenever I wore make-up. Mind you, Emily knew that I had issues in regards to my weight.

I'd spend hours professing my feelings to her and once her cup was full things would go back to normal, only to repeat once her cup was empty.

To make matters worse, Emily's mother made it more challenging by filling her head with the idea that I was only dating her because I had no family. Ugh, why is having no family considered a red flag? Isn't the purpose of developing a relationship to create a family of your own?

Needless to say, I had no time to grieve. My attention was constantly on salvaging Emily's opinion of me.

One night on our way home from a few drinks with her friends, Emily started to cry and told me, 'You're the only one who knows me, Saff,' then proceeded to state, 'My friends don't know the real me.'

I like to believe that this was the real Emily unfiltered, despite what she was putting me through. I genuinely believe that, deep down, she just didn't feel worthy or good enough, so she resorted to toxic methods in order to maintain control. I understand her now in retrospect – though personally I choose to remain vulnerable whenever I feel powerless or unworthy. Everyone handles things in their own way, though. It's just unfortunate that I met her during the worst time of my life. There were two sides to her personality, but the negative side always won.

The final straw was when I couldn't even send a text message around her because she'd accuse me of cheating on her. It was becoming very uncomfortable and my anxiety was through the roof.

It became so bad that my gut started screaming at me to leave, to escape. There had to be a better relationship than this. I knew I had to be brave and return home. I also knew that no matter what I did, I'd always remain the villain. I knew I didn't deserve that title. Nobody saw how she treated me behind closed doors. I just couldn't carry her insecurities on top of my grief anymore.

It was hard to organise anything, though, with Emily watching my every move. As I wasn't allowed on my phone, I took it into the bathroom when she wasn't looking and asked a friend help me book a motel room for the night, then buy me a train ticket back to Sydney for the following day. I strategically packed my two bags and placed them outside when she wasn't looking. I was so nervous – I didn't know what to expect, but I got out.

I was in such a state when I hopped off the train upon arrival in Sydney that I accidently stepped out in front of a child. Despite the fact that I didn't even bump the child and it was a simple accident, her mother yelled at me and called me every name under the sun. What can I say, I was sleep deprived and hungry. My nervous system was shattered.

I remember crying in relief as I entered my motel room. I felt traumatised. Emily and her friends proceeded to send messages detailing how worthless I was.

After checking out of the motel, I found myself homeless in Sydney. I asked Irene and her boyfriend if they could take me in for a week. They agreed and I slept on a blow-up bed on the floor. To express my gratitude, I bought them their favourite alcohol, chocolates, a bunch of flowers and a card.

Within that week I scored myself a part time job at a café,

and scattered Mum's ashes over her favourite beach. I also had two gigs, two demo recordings and I looked for more permanent accommodation.

I also endured more toxic messages from Emily. Irene's boyfriend had a go at me for being on government support and further suggested that I was using and abusing Irene. Oh, and I received a hoax email from a scammer informing me that I was wanted by the federal police. I was going through hell … I felt so hated and unwanted by a lot of people. I will state, though, that Irene defended me when her boyfriend made those suggestions. She was a good friend to me during this time.

In regards to Emily, I don't believe she ever meant to be so abusive. She just allowed fear to dictate her emotions and therefore projected some toxic methods into our relationship as a result. But hey, don't forget we're only human.

Emily was enough.

I was enough.

We just weren't right for one another … again, that's okay!

I forgive Emily … even if she isn't sorry.

In regards to myself, I'm bloody proud of the fact that I conquered such adversity with sheer grace and determination! I don't believe I have anything to be sorry for.

Chapter 10

It Gets Worse

It was becoming very clear that I didn't belong in Sydney anymore. I was fired when I returned back to work. Luckily, Sharon called and told me that her uncle in Melbourne was looking for a new housemate and asked if I'd like his spare room. It was meant to be! Without hesitation, I agreed to take it. So I paid her uncle two weeks' bond upfront, and moved to Melbourne.

I recall feeling incredibly elated as I boarded the train to Melbourne. I carried two bags, my Casio keyboard and hope in my heart. I was at peace with my decision.

Upon my arrival, Sharon greeted me at the train station and drove me to her uncle's house. He lived in a modest two bedroom home in the western suburbs. He was your typical Aussie bloke with a one-year-old baby. I recall him saying, 'Babies are very healing to be around.' I knew that I was in safe hands.

During the first few weeks, Sharon and I hung out quite often, and it wasn't too long until we became intimate again. Emily contacted me during this time and accused me of cheating on her with Sharon once it was revealed that we were seeing each other. I was merely friends with Sharon during my time with Emily – despite what she thinks – but I can see how it appeared at the time and I acknowledge how that would've hurt Emily.

I'd never anticipated going there again in regards to Sharon. I'd only viewed her from a platonic perspective since our last encounter, and never intended to revisit that chapter of my life – but when you're vulnerable, these things can happen. However, the nature of my connection with Sharon was similar to my connection with Emily. It was almost as if Sharon had replicated everything I'd told her about that experience. Her intentions baffled me. She'd project a lot onto me and put me in some hurtful situations. I'd always have to justify everything to her to earn her trust. I remember her sitting in the car with me one day and telling me, 'I should've made you do it all on your own, Saff.' She was also pursuing and hung up on another girl, who she kept sleeping with. It was doomed to end within the space of three weeks.

Don't get me wrong, Sharon was an awesome human being. But when it came to anything remotely intimate between us, it set off the worst in her. Granted, I still had some self-discovery to do in regards to myself. Thankfully, Sharon's uncle was very laidback and I didn't lose my room as a result of the breakup.

Once Sharon was gone, I had no one. I remember feeling so alone. Imagine not having one person in your phone list who'll accept your call, and having absolutely no support system two months into a period of grief. It was utter torture! I spent many nights crying myself to sleep. My anxiety got so bad that I started to experience intense vertigo to the point the entire room would spin. It was pretty scary.

Some good news would arrive, though. I managed to score myself a full-time job as a receptionist and I started to get some paid gigs at a few trendy bars.

Some things were starting to fall into place but, in regards to my love life, I started to give up on the quest. I embraced my solitude by going to the movies by myself, and I signed up for the gym in order to occupy my spare time.

One day I was just about to delete my online dating account, then boom, good old Lilly appeared. Lilly was a 39-year-old unemployed country bumpkin with a cheeky sense of humour. As bad as it may sound, I wasn't attracted to her – but proceeded to give her a chance because we had some good banter. I invited Lilly to attend one of my gigs, but her enthusiasm was practically non-existent once I'd finished my set. Instead, she just stared at me awkwardly as she waited for a mutual connection to arrive. This didn't feel right to me, though I never acknowledged my feelings at the time.

Most of my encounters with Lilly centred around frustrations toward her ex and just how broken she was.

(Lilly's ex left her for another woman). It never occurred to me that Lilly wasn't over her. A lot of anger surfaced towards this ex through our discussions, but I shrugged it off knowing that I've also held onto anger toward an ex due to similar reasons. After all, we're only human. These things take time.

As time passed, I noticed that Lilly wasn't someone who cared for you whenever you were sick. I recall having gastro/food poisoning twice while in Lilly's company, and she slept all the way through my symptoms. When I woke up, she chuckled in response to my misfortune.

She wasn't very supportive of my emotional wellbeing either in regards to the loss of my mother – though a part of me chose to overlook these factors.

I made a foolish mistake of quitting my job and moving to the country to spend more time with her. Hey, I was vulnerable. These things happen. It wasn't too long, however, until I scored myself a part-time job.

Lilly and I would drink with her friends on most weekends. I won't lie, it was a lot of fun and it allowed me to escape all that I'd previously endured.

Around this time, Lilly's ex-girlfriend came back into the picture, and Lilly started to question if she was still in love with her. I confronted Lilly about her true feelings, and watched as Lilly pondered her thoughts. She said, 'I'm not just with you because you look good on paper,' then, 'If I choose her, she'll just choose the other girl, and I'll be alone again'.

I stood back in utter shock. I mean, she'd practically inferred that I was just a second option, a back-up plan. At the time, I thought this was just karma teaching me a lesson for what I did to Soozie, when really I was attracting situations that challenged my sense of self-worth. For some reason, though, I continued to date her. I think we were both so alone and vulnerable that we just fell into a dysfunctional relationship.

I found myself always being compared to Lilly's ex. Lilly would also suggest things such as, 'You'd get my attention if you wore more tightly-fitted clothing or if you dyed your hair darker.' She had a tendency to 'look over the fence' in regards to other women. One night at a club, Lilly cuddled into a girl and told her, 'You smell so good' with a cheeky grin. When I addressed it, she said that I was being 'too sensitive', though when I asked if she was attracted to this girl, Lilly responded, 'Yes.' I proceeded to ask Lilly if she was attracted to me. She responded, 'Yes, but you're no model.'

Lilly continued to speak to this girl online. I looked at her messages (because I didn't trust her) and noticed that Lilly was flirting with her. I have no shame for looking at Lilly's phone, and I'd do it again. Under these circumstances you need confirmation of your doubts, otherwise you're just wasting your time in that relationship. Nevertheless, it was very clear that Lilly wasn't happy with me and that she was indeed looking for a way out. Despite these factors, I still continued to date her.

I started to project my fears and anxieties regarding Lilly whenever we'd drink with her friends. I didn't feel safe with her, but nobody understood where I was coming from. I mean, let's be honest, when you're drunk you're not in the best position to articulate yourself. I wasn't the best drunk, and I wasn't very respectful to her friends. But deep down, a lot of my crap surfaced because I felt as if nobody liked me. Truth be told, I really liked her friends and I just wanted to be understood and accepted.

Once I realised that I had some underlying issues, I attempted to work on myself. I started to listen to positive affirmations in order to improve my confidence, because I knew that I wouldn't be subjecting myself to this mental torture if I truly loved myself.

Despite my best efforts, I couldn't help but feel trapped and alone. I started seeking new friends in the LGBT community online because I had no emotional support. But if I'm truly being honest, I may've subconsciously been seeking a way out of the relationship.

Out of the blue, a man named Rob came across my music page on social media and approached me to become my music manager. Rob had a friend who offered to record my first EP, but the genre had to be rock & roll because that's all he knew how to produce, which was a fair compromise in order for my music to be heard.

To add to my small successes, my music was featured in a lesbian magazine. I was also invited to perform at a music convention. I offered Lilly an opportunity to be one of my backup singers because I wanted her to feel included in the project. When we arrived, I received a VIP pass. Lilly was furious and proceeded to state, 'Oh it's okay, I'm not worthy of a VIP pass.' So I gave her mine, which she accepted.

By this stage, I really wanted to end my connection with Lilly but I had no way out, and when I did I'd make excuses out of guilt for leaving her behind. I truly cared about her, but it got to a point where I couldn't drown with her.

Around this time, I was offered an opportunity to record my first music video in Adelaide. Prior to leaving, I recall having high anxiety that Lilly would sabotage my experience.

The videographers were friends with my manager and welcomed us into their home. I bought them flowers and chocolates in appreciation.

When we arrived, Lilly was antisocial towards everyone and locked herself in our room for the entire weekend. In hindsight, I understand that she felt inadequate. But at the time, I attempted to involve her in the project and her lack of support hurt me. She didn't even try. To be fair, I didn't consider from her perspective how it would feel to watch someone become more successful than you, and because she'd already put me through so much I had very little tolerance for her behaviour.

Some people would say that jealousy is a curse, but I beg to differ. I like to believe that jealousy is merely a representation of where someone feels something lacking within themselves. It's never personal, even though it may feel like it is at times. Some people genuinely believe that they cannot attain what you have.

I'm speaking from personal experience in relation to both ends of the spectrum. I'm in no way suggesting that you should tolerate or subject yourself to anyone who projects their past onto you within a relationship. They need to be willing to work through their insecurities in a constructive manner using quality communication. You should always make your own needs and feelings your first priority ... but in the realm of detaching yourself from a person with these underlining issues, who is in a vulnerable and delicate state, the best way forward is to be kind and compassionate towards them. I mean, they already feel worthless. People may continue to resent and hate you, but at least you're not negatively contributing to the situation.

The videographers spoke to me in private regarding the state of my relationship and told me I could do better. For once, I was in the position of being 'the catch.' It definitely gave me a boost of confidence, that's for sure!

On the final night of our stay in Adelaide, we were at a party with the videographers and their friends. Lilly pulled me aside and picked a fight with me. She said, 'I'm not a rock star – it's okay, I'll just be your bag carrier.' Funnily enough, though, I was actually *her* bag carrier. I reminded Lilly that I'd done everything possible to support her dreams and endeavours. All that I wanted in return was a little respect.

I watched as Lilly continued the night with consideration for everyone else and complete disregard toward me. I looked back at all the times she'd go out of her way to demonstrate her enthusiasm toward strangers, yet she never displayed an ounce of care-factor in regards to me. I also recalled the times when she'd write poetry for strangers who never once lifted a finger for her. Yet here I was, bending over backwards to make her feel truly loved and appreciated, while she never once did the same for me.

Considering what she'd put me through, I was bloody terrific to her. I never once raised any of her weaknesses or flaws. I'd always made allowances for her up until this point. It was the same old story and it was time for me to re-evaluate my sense of value! I just wanted out! (See what happens when you get a boost of validation regarding your worth!)

The videographers offered me a place to stay if I decided to end things with Lilly. It was upon that offer that I made up my mind, but I didn't act on my decision until we returned back to Melbourne. Once Lilly and I were home, I ended my connection with her. I recall holding her hand with tears in my eyes as I said, 'I hope that you love yourself one day.' I left the following day.

I knew that Lilly would struggle to sit in uncomfortable truths and take some ownership over how the break-up transpired – and I was prepared to be thrown under the bus as a result. She portrayed herself as the victim on social media. I understand that sometimes you just need the support of your friends, even when you're somewhat at fault. Let's just say that growing pains aren't easy, and I understand why people avoid enduring them.

On the way home from Adelaide, I decided to message my friend Anna, who I'd met while I was with Soozie. Anna had come to live in Melbourne prior to me and I'd occupied her old room in Sydney before I too moved to Melbourne. Her mother had recently moved to Melbourne in order to support her, and they shared a three bedroom house. It was arranged that I'd occupy their spare room once I returned, just for a few days.

I then travelled back to Adelaide to regroup and stayed with the videographers for three weeks, where I hung out more with Belinda, who'd played an additional character in my music video. Belinda was a straight 25-year-old woman with substance, empathy and goals. We'd bonded instantly. The video had required Belinda to step outside her comfort zone and play a gay woman in a dysfunctional gay-relationship. I will admit, I was attracted to her.

Before I knew it, Belinda and I were intimate. I never anticipated that outcome given Belinda was straight, but if I'm honest, I'd started to like her from the very first day we met. Look at me, I technically emotionally cheated in a relationship, having reached out to Belinda while Lilly and I were still together. Now the shoe was on the other foot. I don't condone cheating – but if someone refuses to make an effort to treat you better in a relationship, these things might happen.

Sadly, my time with Belinda was short lived as the connection was similar to many of my other dysfunctional connections. Don't get me wrong, Belinda was a great woman who I truly admired. We both had a lot of growing to do, though!

In regards to the videographers, it became clear that my connection with Belinda annoyed them – as they advised me on many occasions to remain single for a while to work on myself. They were right, but hey, you don't learn these lessons until you learn them. Nevertheless, I'm grateful that they took me in for those three weeks. They were the catalyst for me detaching from another dysfunctional connection.

In regards to Lilly, her projections were a representation of how inadequate she felt. It was never personal and I can see that now – because I can relate to those feelings and I understand the anxiety that transpires as a result.

I never once asked her to get a job, to clean her house or to alter her appearance. I just wanted her love and support. But unfortunately at the time Lilly was still haunted by her past. She simply valued the wrong things based on a belief system that money, superficiality and materialistic attainment would attribute to her sense of self-worth – and as a consequence she lost a good thing.

Deep down, she was enough.

I was enough.

We just weren't right for each other.

I hope that Lilly found the love that she truly deserves, and accepts it!

I forgive Lilly, even if she isn't sorry. I also forgive myself for my own shortcomings and for emotionally cheating on her.

Chapter 11

Growing Pains

When I returned to Melbourne Rob had a band lined up for me. I'd attend weekly rehearsals in a proper studio and we'd all evenly distribute the cost. It worked out to be ten dollars per person, which is a fantastic rate for band practice. My band members were much older and they were happy to play for free, as I was strapped for cash because I couldn't attain stable employment due to moving around so much. Needless to say, my resume was very flaky.

Within two months of my return to Melbourne, Anna's mother asked me to move out as she wasn't coping in regards to sharing with other people. She would regularly comment on minor details and was irritable most of the time. Mind you, I was a very respectful housemate – I paid my rent in advance, I was generous whenever she was depressed, I cleaned the house and I kept to myself. Despite these positive factors, I respected her wishes and left the following day. In hindsight, I understand where Anna's mum was coming from. She was unemployed and she was trying to find her place in the workforce all over again. This can take its toll on a person. She had every right to feel this way, though at the time I felt discarded and unwanted.

I woke up with a mission to find a new place and found one close by. Within an hour of moving in, though, my new housemate informed me that her ex-boyfriend had just got out of prison, and that he'd be making unwanted visits from time to time. I recall trembling as I experienced immediate flashbacks to my childhood. I was in absolutely no state to endure this all over again. I picked up my bags and hiked a thirty minute walk in the blazing heat to a beach nearby.

I messaged Anna to tell her what had happened and she replied, 'Wow'. It appeared as if she didn't care, so I refrained from asking her if I could come back and stay for a couple of days. I was homeless again. I remember sitting on the beach (surrounded by my two bags and Casio keyboard) in absolute tears. I peered out onto the ocean as I pondered my future. I contemplated sleeping there for the night because I had no money to check into a motel.

I sent Rob a text message and practically begged him to ask his parents if they'd let me stay for a short while as they had a spare room. Thankfully, an hour later Rob messaged me to say his parents had agreed to take me in until I found permanent accommodation.

During this time, I felt quite vulnerable and called my dad for the first time in years. I told him that Mum had passed away and that she'd always spoken fondly of him. I proceeded to tell him that I held no resentment for what happened. He wasn't very understanding in his response, but he was relatively pleasant despite his lack of regard. We never spoke again. I was completely alone.

I went on a few dates, though they all turned out to be the same. It was as if everyone that I came across wanted to alter something about me. I was at a point where I wasn't willing to compromise myself anymore for anyone, so I just focused on my music.

The band and I scored ourselves a lot of gigs and I had a lot of fun with everyone – though I wasn't emotionally connected to the musical genre of rock and roll. I just loved goofing around with everyone.

I persisted for a few months, but I was miserable despite any positive feedback. Some days were really hard. I cried a lot, especially during rehearsals. I was contending with numerous other factors that were causing me to crack under the pressure.

Despite the band's best efforts to cheer me up, my self-worth had decreased yet again and I lacked any motivation to move forward. I felt like a lost cause and started to experience suicidal thoughts. Sure, I didn't have a job, I didn't have a permanent address and I had no family… but why should that determine my worthiness to remain on this planet? Why would it be deemed impossible for me to experience a good outcome? It was becoming very apparent that the only person who could save me was myself, so I decided to hold on and fight for my life!

During this time, Belinda attempted to come back into the picture, but I remained adamant that I was onto a good thing.

I started to stay in hostels on the weekends and I'd socialise with many backpackers. I was conditioning myself to a new way of life.

Rob's mother was truly a blessing during this time. She'd wash my clothes and then neatly fold them upon my bed. She'd also go out of her own way to make me hot cups of tea whenever I was sick. Rob's mother reminded me a lot of my mum, and this made me miss her even more. I recall crying in appreciation and I bought her flowers as a gesture of my gratitude.

In regards to Rob, we had some confrontations but our differences only strengthened me and made me more determined to remain true to myself. Ultimately, I believe his only intention was to make me stronger. Rob was a good man and I recall having many good times with him.

Once I'd shifted my sense of self-worth, suddenly Marilyn came into my life when I wasn't even looking. Marilyn was an ex of an old acquaintance I'd met via a dating app when I initially moved to Melbourne. I was introduced to her briefly during my relationship with Lilly – though I never anticipated that I'd end up dating her in the near future.

Marilyn's ex had described her as someone who had a devious personality and was a bit of a player, so I purposely avoided any association with her. However, throughout a few discussions I detected a different side to Marilyn, and concluded that Marilyn's ex might have skewed the truth post breakup. When we believe only one version of a story, this is how we miss out on opportunities.

Marilyn gave me the fairytale that I was seeking. She was perfect and would be my first proper relationship in terms of intimacy and communication. It would be anything but smooth sailing, though, as we had to navigate quite a few past traumas together, but she was devoted to working through it with me. Still, we didn't properly commit until months into our development.

Some of my band members established that I wasn't happy with my current musical direction, and they advised to follow my heart. Within two weeks, I had moved in with Marilyn, quit the band and ended my professional relationship with Rob. I just wanted to run away and start afresh.

During the first month of my relationship with Marilyn, Belinda messaged and professed her love to me, despite knowing that I was in a relationship. She travelled to

Melbourne to see me, but it was too late. I had fallen for Marilyn and I wasn't going to jeopardise a good thing.

I decided to try out a new career direction, so I commenced studies in TV/Film and joined a talent agency. I worked as a TV extra, playing a police woman, a nurse and a recovering drug addict, but the gigs didn't last and I wasn't getting any further despite my best efforts.

I went on to explore electronic music and recorded more demos. I sent my songs to a bunch of music publishers only to be declined. I then decided to take a leap of faith and applied for a talent show. I got through to the first round of auditions, only to be eliminated in the second round. To cut a long story short, I failed everything!

Marilyn was a successful business woman with a very supportive and functional family. I'd be lying if I said that I didn't struggle with that. Seeing her success only heightened my feelings of worthlessness and I missed my mum. Marilyn deserved everything that she achieved, but it made me more conscious of the fact that I hadn't had that kind of support, and was doing everything on my own. I just needed to look at things from a different perspective. These things take time.

To make matters worse, a lot of people believed that I was a gold digger and that I wasn't good enough for Marilyn, that she was the 'special' one. I never understood why both of us couldn't be considered special.

Even though I'd finally received the love I deserved, it didn't come without obstacles. I was ridiculed for my choice of career. 'She has no money,' they'd say, among many other hurtful comments. I was also ridiculed for my body issues, trust issues, abandonment issues and my lack of self-worth. I just couldn't get an easy run. I found myself empathising with a few of my exes and what had compelled them to go back to their coping mechanisms. I understood them so much more during this stage of my growth. I even messaged Lilly and I apologised for my shortcomings.

When you feel inadequate, it's difficult to suppress that level of intense emotion. I never wanted Marilyn to be subjected to the mental and emotional torture that I'd experienced, so I kept my shit together. I mean, I couldn't say to Marilyn, 'Hey, can you stop being so successful, because it's making me uncomfortable?' Instead, I relied upon a healthier form of communication and tried to be honest but respectful, not project my feelings onto her. I'd acknowledge how proud I was of her, but refrain from jealous thoughts. I'll admit, communication can prove challenging when two people are coming from opposite perspectives. But if you're willing to open your mind and work at it, it's worthwhile.

One of the biggest lessons I learned during this difficult time was that you have to gently fight for your truth without carrying any shame for being vulnerable. Putting your walls up only makes things harder. You should never yell nor should you attack someone just to make your point. Always share your perspective with kindness. Sure, some people may use your vulnerability against you. But at least you'll know that you've been your authentic self in a relationship. There's true strength in vulnerability. Ego only wounds you in the end.

I also learned that even your soulmate will hurt you. Don't expect smooth sailing all of the way. There are complexities to contend with when joining forces with someone who's a polar opposite to you. It's important to allow each other to have weaknesses. After all, nobody is perfect. If someone is right for you, they'll work with you.

I had to sit in a lot of uncomfortable truths during this phase of my development. It wasn't easy. I cried almost every day and had to fight many mental and emotional battles in the process. I constantly compared myself to other girls and I devalued what I brought to the table in a relationship. I couldn't give myself any credit. I never hated the women I felt threatened by – I was merely concerned that my partner might like them more than me, because that's all I'd been subjected to prior to my relationship with Marilyn.

I started to realise that I was rather damaged and became aware of my hypersensitivity during social interactions. Granted, sometimes it was merited, based on indirect insinuations presented to me on numerous occasions. Some days were so incredibly difficult that I contemplated giving up on the relationship because I didn't feel like I was enough. It's a daily struggle to feel like you're enough in this world. I won't pretend that the journey toward self-love is easy, hence why so many relationships fall apart. Nevertheless, I didn't want to react to my triggers, so I started to see a psychologist. It was a very wise choice, which helped managed my anxiety.

A part of me can now see the value of all that I've experienced and I'm grateful for the failures as they've encouraged me to grow. I've also learnt just how resilient I am. I've survived some remarkable events!

In regards to my relationship with Marilyn, we were on and off again over the course of the first two years. She was my first true love. We're best friends now, and I have a greater understanding of myself and what I need when it comes to my relationships thanks to all of my broken ones. In the end, we were forced to break up due to extenuating circumstances, but continue to remain good friends to this day. I'm eternally grateful for Marilyn and I've learned a great deal during our time together. I believe she is my soulmate. One day there might be a time to reconnect romantically, but for now I'm just working on myself. I'd like to believe that we'll last forever, though it's never guaranteed. But I do have faith.

In regards to my music, I started to write new songs and went back to my roots performing at Open Mic nights … but I still have some work to do in regards to improving the way I perceive myself. One thing was certain, I was writing better songs and my new direction entailed an intention to create a more positive effect on humanity. I was no longer singing about heartbreak and bitterness. I was writing songs about the true essence of personal growth throughout the adversity I was enduring. Regardless if I made it or not, I was moving forward in a more constructive direction.

A part of me suspects my previous intentions to pursue music were indeed for the wrong reasons. With time, though, I realised that no amount of success will ever fill the void in combatting self-worth ... that's an entirely different ballgame! All the people I wanted to prove wrong and display my worthiness to wouldn't have cared either way. If people are already against you, why would success change their perception of you!? And if it did, would it be for the right reasons? Perhaps not!

Music will always be a part of my journey, but to keep my options open, I took up full-time studies as a counsellor and became fully qualified. Counselling has taught me a great deal about the human condition and how particular events can impact a person, leading to many social, mental and emotional complexities. I've developed a greater tolerance and compassion toward people as a result.

It also inspired me to reconnect with a few acquaintances and friends from my past. I realised that everyone had their own family and friends to focus on, though, and I felt more alone as a result. Don't get me wrong, those people are wonderful – they just had their own family and friends to care about, and that's completely fair. They aren't responsible for my wellbeing, nor should they be.

I don't know what my future holds ... but hey, I've come this far.

Chapter 12

Perspective

Some people have strong opinions, and those strong opinions are generally verbalised as judgments which ultimately affect how we see ourselves, and can cause us to either change or punish ourselves. Some people will work extremely hard to prove their worth via the means of success, only to discover it made no difference in the eyes of the person who originally questioned it. They never needed to prove themselves, anyway. Meanwhile on the other hand, other people may end up settling for what they believe they deserve, only to endure some negative consequences as a result. It's a double-edged sword.

Some people would go so far to suggest that you shouldn't remain a victim of your past, but let's not forget that everyone has their own learning styles, and people are more complex than we allow them credit for. If you're continually judged based on face value, it's inevitable you'll start to doubt yourself and make decisions based on a misconception. Power of suggestion is just that – powerful, though dangerous to an impressionable mind! Imagine what we could all achieve if all our feedback was positive? Then again, some of our biggest failures end up being our biggest wins in the end.

These days, I attempt to challenge the noise inside my head. I question and challenge all those little voices of doubt. With every response they spit back, the answers become weaker and more ridiculous. Opinions are gradually losing their power over me, though it's daily work! I mean, I've constantly been deemed worthless for being poor and having no family. Meanwhile other people are being defined as worthless for other factors, such as living at home with their parents, struggling to kick their addictions and for being single, etc. Really? Why are things like human compassion and acts of kindness less favoured, while status, appearance and money still determine our worth? Have we learned nothing? Shouldn't the quality of a person be defined by the state of their humanity? Imagine if our society collapsed and we reverted back to the days of cavemen. How would we survive? Better yet, how would we redefine ourselves without status, appearance and money? I suspect it would be one massive shit-storm.

If I've learnt anything from losing everything, it's that attaching myself to things and people in order to feel secure always fails, because things and people aren't permanent.

I've also learnt that changing for someone else doesn't mean they'll change their behaviour. They'll always find a fault within you because they haven't addressed the issues within themselves. Embrace your authenticity, and forgive those people with compassion for their weaknesses.

I want to finish this book by stating that everyone upon my journey was more than enough! My main purpose in writing this story has been to illustrate where some of us tend to go wrong regarding our observations and judgements. We immediately deem people as lost causes and toxic if they don't fit with what we perceive to be orthodox or normal. Some people are just struggling to survive, and resort to what they need to in order to manage their fear. Not everyone is going to react well to fear – but it doesn't make someone a bad person for doing so. Granted, in some cases I can understand why it would be difficult to forgive someone, as it's completely merited.

On another note, I believe calling someone a loser due to their lack of motivation is counterproductive and only wounds people in the end. Nothing positive can be attained by putting other people down. Some of the people labelled as losers have already given up on themselves. They don't need to be subjected to any more torment.

On my journey I have won and I have lost. I understand how it feels from both perspectives. It would be wonderful if we could all display a little compassion in regards to why people are the way they are and just let people be, if they're not affecting you personally. All we need to do is apply a little patience toward others and ourselves in our daily proceedings.

You know that person in the check-out line who is giving you a death stare as they telepathically tell you to hurry up? Or that person tooting you on the highway for cutting into their lane? Or that one friend who unintentionally insulted you regarding your bad haircut? And what about that person who gossiped about you, without any consideration to your side to the story? Well that's you, too – on a completely different day!

If we were all monitored 24/7, we'd discover we display these tendencies within ourselves. We're anything but perfect and hey, that's okay!

The trick is to be more considerate with everyone's feelings, choices, authenticities and struggles, and forgive them of their shortcomings as you would for yourself. Again, I do understand that forgiveness is a hard thing to muster and I still have days where I fall short. But it's in the trying that counts!

True self-love isn't attained easily. I suspect that true self-love is where you can sit in your failures whilst sipping your cup of coffee and you're prepared to embrace the rain.

I don't believe you need anything in this world in order to justify your worth. I like to believe that a higher power loves us all in the end.

Chapter 13

2020

Interesting fact – Covid-19 occurred just weeks after I wrote this book, providing a great opportunity for self-reflection. I think a lot of people could relate to how small most of us felt during the crisis. I think when we all think of 2020, we associate it with great turbulence, and a deep set of wounds and traumas that impacted our lives forevermore.

In my case, I had been undergoing intense psychological assistance. For the first time in my life, I saw a psychiatrist in order to get a professional diagnosis of what I was contending with. It can be really difficult to seek assistance. Some people don't help you during the diagnosis period – not everyone is going to make it an easy ride for you. But it's important to stick it out. Don't allow yourself to be treated like another number. Your health is important. Fight for the right assistance for you.

It turned out that I'd been contending with complex post-traumatic syndrome disorder (PTSD) since the age of five. I was also advised that I had generalised anxiety and a panic disorder, only to top it off with an obsessive compulsive personality disorder. Wow, what a thing to sit in during Melbourne's extreme lockdown.

I was prescribed various medications to combat the immense stress my body was under. I couldn't sleep without experiencing night terrors regarding aspects of my past and the people in it. Sometimes I'd be attacked or faced with people from my childhood who really tormented me. Everything was being presented to me and I had very little support. I really had to dissect the dreams and work with a counsellor and psychologist to make sense of why my dreams were so rich. It was hard work and I won't lie, sometimes I still experience them. It's a daily battle.

The kidnap letters had been the primary issue. It explained my fear of going to school, and with further unpacking I came to understand that was why I was still technically a virgin, as I have a great fear of penetration. All this time I was dressing as a tomboy in fear of men looking at me. I realised I am very feminine and learned to embrace it without fear. That's how complex my PTSD is. Imagine that, a 34 year-old virgin because I associate sex with pain due to the context of those letters.

It also explains my need for perfectionism and my need to overcompensate when someone appears disappointed or silent with me. It makes perfect sense now.

I also experienced night terrors regarding my mum. I'd experience dreams of her death and going through the entire sequence of events that transpired, in regards to her passing, all over again.

Some nights I'd dream that I was arguing with her in relation to how she raised me, and the trauma that I now have to heal as a result of her care. I'd almost resent her for leaving me behind, especially knowing that I healed her before she passed away.

It was a dark time in my mind. I was questioning everything around me. Nothing felt real anymore. But with much unpacking and comparison regarding my own inability to practice perfection, I realised I may of done the same with such little resources. Therefore I was able to forgive the situations I grew up in and forgive my mum for not knowing any other way.

Looking back in hindsight, I can see my mother had mental illness herself. Based on my studies I'd suggest she'd also had complex PTSD, anxiety, agoraphobia and avoidance issues. Considering her illness, though, she did a great job in raising me, and taught me to never judge anyone.

All the people who labelled me as crazy and problematic might be sitting with some great reflection as to how misunderstood I've been throughout my entire life. I have so much gratitude for my failures. They've built my character and resistance. The chips will fall as they may.

I decided to quit singing, but intend to focus on counselling and mental health so that I can continue to help others with similar issues to what I have, help them feel less alone. Everyone you meet is struggling with the same issues, self-worth and heartaches.

During Christmas I'd go to visit homeless people and give them groceries, help elderly people when they couldn't afford toilet paper due to shortages, and sent care packages to people who'd been there for me. I wanted to give back, and that felt more rewarding than anything.

On my Mum's birthday I gave a woman flowers. I just knew intuitively that she was a selfless woman rushing home to tend to everyone else's needs before thinking of herself. She said her dad died years ago, and had promised he'd always give her a sign that he'd never forget her. This was a sign.

She said, 'He's watching over me,' and cried as she accepted the flowers. It filled my heart knowing I could still give someone flowers on Mum's birthday – my favourite thing to do.

So that sums it up for now. As I previously said in my introduction, this isn't a story about being entirely healed. It's a journey of unpacking, doing the work, and understanding where your triggers stem from in order to gain more self-awareness and prevent repeating the cycle.

It's basically a story about someone who remains in the process of healing. So hey, let's heal together and support each other when we have setbacks. Life is very unpredictable, and saying that you're 100% healed is only setting yourself up for failure. It's daily practice and it requires support.

2020

I've had a heck of a year. I fractured two of my rib cartilage that I'm about to undergo surgery for, I have an overactive thyroid and low blood sugar. I've lost ten kilos and I've endured a lot of night terrors, along with night sweats. It's been hell. But I'm choosing to hold on and remain grateful for my blessings. I can rise above this.

I want anyone who is considering giving up to know that your life has meaning, you are enough and one day it will all make sense.

You're not alone and this isn't the end. These growing pains are just turning us into the people we wish to be – heroes!

Don't lose hope. Don't give up. Heal with me.

To conclude my book, some people are really hurting out there, and I hope that this story can help somebody to feel less alone with their thoughts and experiences. Be kind to yourself and know that you're enough!

Acknowledgements

I'd like to thank everyone in this book who contributed to my growth, especially my mum. I'd also like to thank my publisher Blaise van Hecke and editor Meg Hellyer at Busybird Publishing.

Resources

If you've been triggered by any of the things discussed in this book, here are some helpful resources.

Lifeline: 13 11 14 or lifeline.org.au
Beyond Blue: 1300 22 46 36 or beyondblue.org.au
Kids Helpline: 1800 55 18 00 or kidshelpline.com.au
Headspace: 1800 650 890 or headspace.org.au

Saffire-Rose
Fletcher

Revive My Life

A Story For the Experienced

Volume 2

In this follow-up to *Maybe I Can Rise Above*, Saffire-Rose Fletcher continues her journey of self-exploration, growth, and spiritual reconciliation.

Battling through tumultuous relationships, the ongoing struggle to build her music career, debilitating and chronic pain that requires two surgeries, a nervous breakdown, withdrawing from prescribed medication, the haunting loss of her mum, and a suicide attempt, all while navigating a global pandemic that shuts her off from all help and recourse, Saffire fights to not only find a place where she belongs, but also a way to move forward.

Revive My Life isn't a self-help book, but a memoir about self-discovery, courage through adversity, and evolution, a must-read for anybody questioning their self-worth, and navigating their way toward rebuilding their life after a dark time.

Don't forget you can find me here ...

Facebook:
www.facebook.com/saffireroseofficial/

Instagram:
www.instagram.com/saffirerosefletcher_official

YouTube:
www.YouTube.com/saffirerosefletcher

www.ingramcontent.com/pod-product-compliance
Lightning Source LLC
Chambersburg PA
CBHW070107120526
44588CB00032B/1369